United States
Department of
Agriculture

Forest Service

**Southern
Research Station**

Resource Bulletin
SRS–94

# North Carolina's Timber Industry— An Assessment of Timber Product Output and Use, 2001

Michael Howell and
David R. Brown

## The Authors:

**Michael Howell** is a Resource Analyst with the Forest
Inventory and Analysis Research Work Unit, Southern
Research Station, U.S. Department of Agriculture, Forest
Service, Knoxville, TN 37919. **David R. Brown** is a State
Forest Supervisor with the North Carolina Department of
Environment, Health, and Natural Resources, Division of
Forest Resources, DuPont State Forest, Cedar Mountain, NC
28718-0300.

May 2004

Southern Research Station
P.O. Box 2680
Asheville, NC 28802

## Foreword

This report contains the findings of a 2001 canvas of all primary wood-using plants in North Carolina, and presents changes in product output and residue use since 1999. It complements the Forest Inventory and Analysis periodic inventory of volume and removals from the State's timberland. The canvass was conducted to determine the amount and source of wood receipts and annual timber product drain, by county, in 2001 and to determine interstate and cross-regional movement of industrial roundwood. Only primary wood-using mills were canvassed. Primary mills are those that process roundwood in log or bolt form or as chipped roundwood. Examples of industrial roundwood products are saw logs, pulpwood, veneer logs, poles, and logs used for composite board products. Mills producing products from residues generated at primary and secondary processors were not canvassed. Trees chipped in the woods were included in the estimate of timber drain only if they were delivered to a primary domestic manufacturer.

A 100-percent canvass of certain wood processors in North Carolina was conducted in 2002 to obtain information for 2001. In addition, roundwood from out-of-State mills known to be using logs or bolts harvested from North Carolina timberland was incorporated into North Carolina production estimates. The mills were canvassed by mail or through personal contact at plant locations. Telephone contacts followed mailed questionnaire responses when additional information or clarification of a response was necessary. In the event of a nonresponse, data collected in previous surveys were updated using current data collected for mills of similar size, product type, and location. Surveys for all timber products other than pulpwood began in 1961, and are currently conducted every 2 years.

Pulpwood production data were taken from an annual canvass of all southern pulpmills. Medium density fiberboard, insulating board, and hardboard plants were included in this survey.

## Acknowledgments

The authors thank Barry D. New for review and comments; Dumitru Salajanu for the maps; Anne Jenkins, Charlene Walker, and Lyn Thornhill for tables, graphs, and statistical checking; and Paul Smith, Diana Corbin, and Louise Wilde for editorial review, styling, and publication of this report.

The Southern Research Station gratefully acknowledges the cooperation and assistance provided by the North Carolina Department of Environment and Natural Resources, Division of Forest Resources in collecting mill data. Appreciation is also extended to forest industry and mill managers for providing timber products information.

# Contents

[a] All tables in this report are available in Microsoft® Excel workbook files. Upon request, these files will be supplied on 3½-inch diskettes.

The use of trade or firm names in this publication is for reader information and does not imply endorsement by the U.S. Department of Agriculture of any product or service.

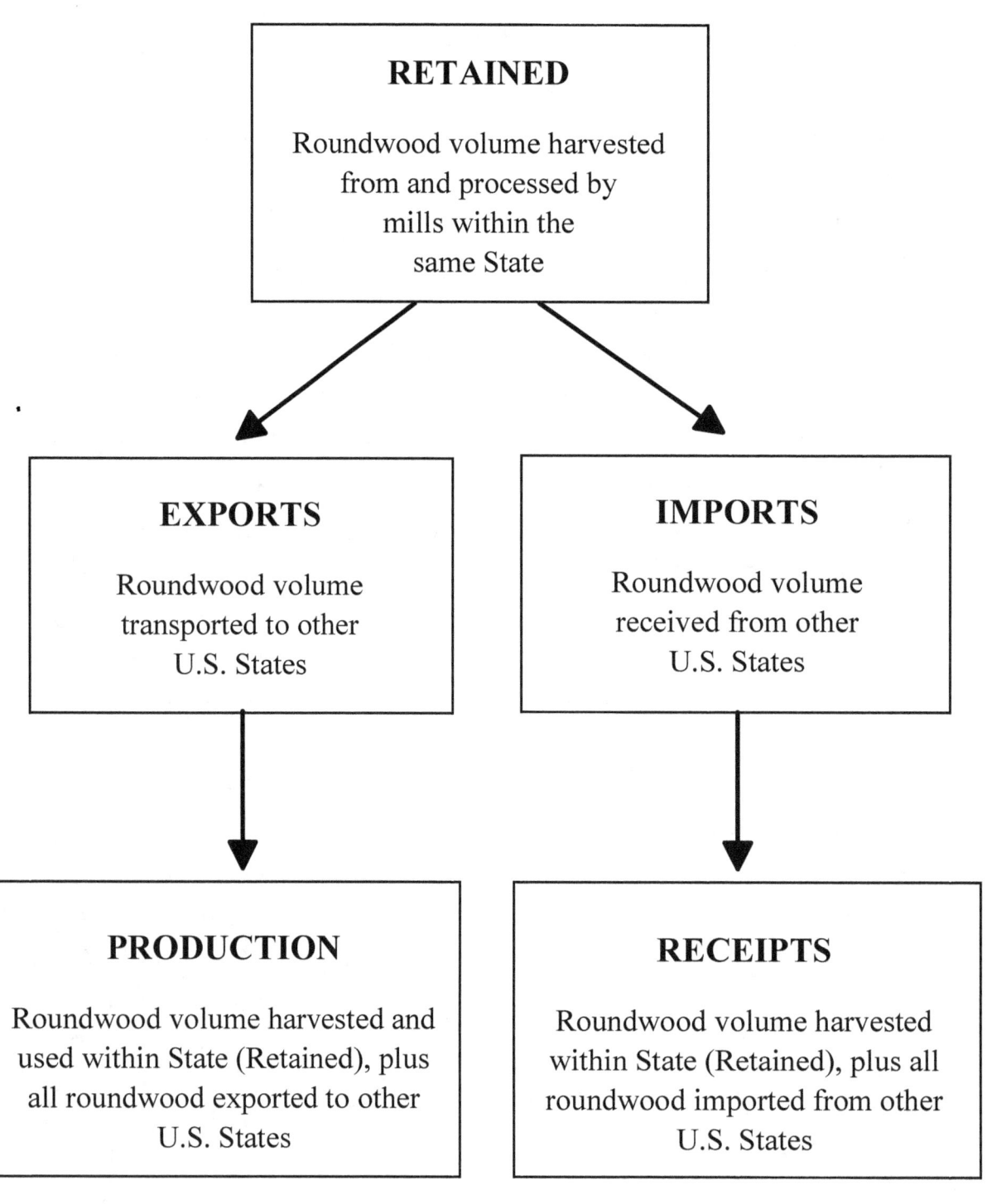

Figure 1—Movement of roundwood exports and imports within the United States.

# North Carolina's Timber Industry—An Assessment of Timber Product Output and Use, 2001

Michael Howell and David R. Brown

## Output of Industrial Timber Products

Note: Certain terms used in this report—retained, export, import, production, and receipts—have specialized meanings unique to the Forest Inventory and Analysis Units across the country that deal with timber products output (fig. 1).

### All Products

- Between 1999 and 2001, the combined industrial timber products output (TPO) from roundwood and plant byproducts declined 3 percent, from 1.10 to 1.07 billion cubic feet.

- TPO from roundwood was down 35 million cubic feet, or 4 percent, to 759 million cubic feet, while output of plant byproducts was up 2.6 million cubic feet to 313 million cubic feet.

- Output of softwood roundwood products declined 4 percent to 512 million cubic feet, while output of hardwood roundwood products dropped 6 percent to 246 million cubic feet (fig. 2).

- Figures 3 and 4 display softwood and hardwood county-level intensity of roundwood production for all industrial products across North Carolina. The data are depicted in cubic feet produced per acre of census land area. Counties with the highest production intensity are depicted in the darker shades. For softwoods the darkest shade represents more than 30 cubic feet of production per acre, while for hardwoods the darkest shade represents more than 15 cubic feet per acre.

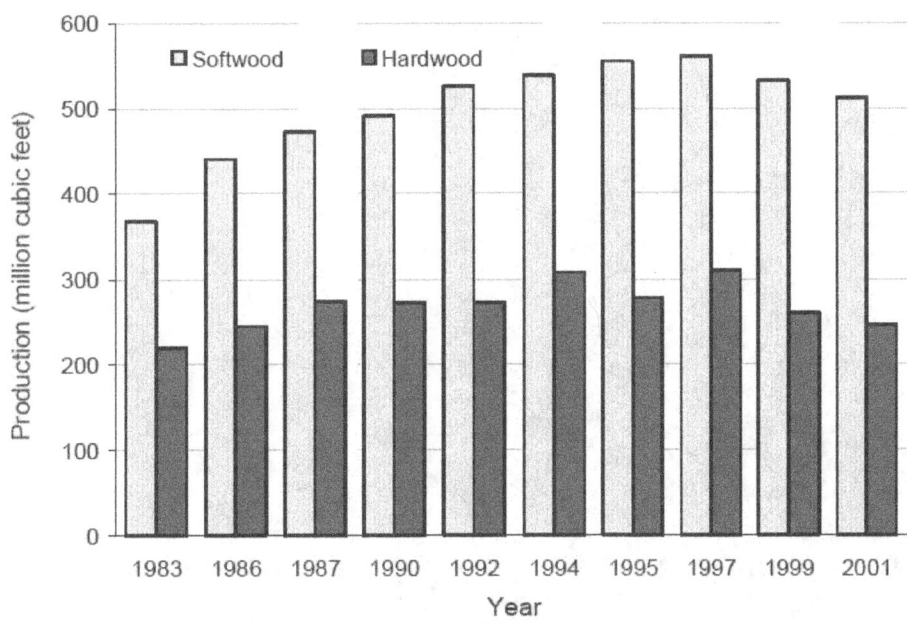

Figure 2—Roundwood production for all products by species group and year (see page 11 for references for individual years).

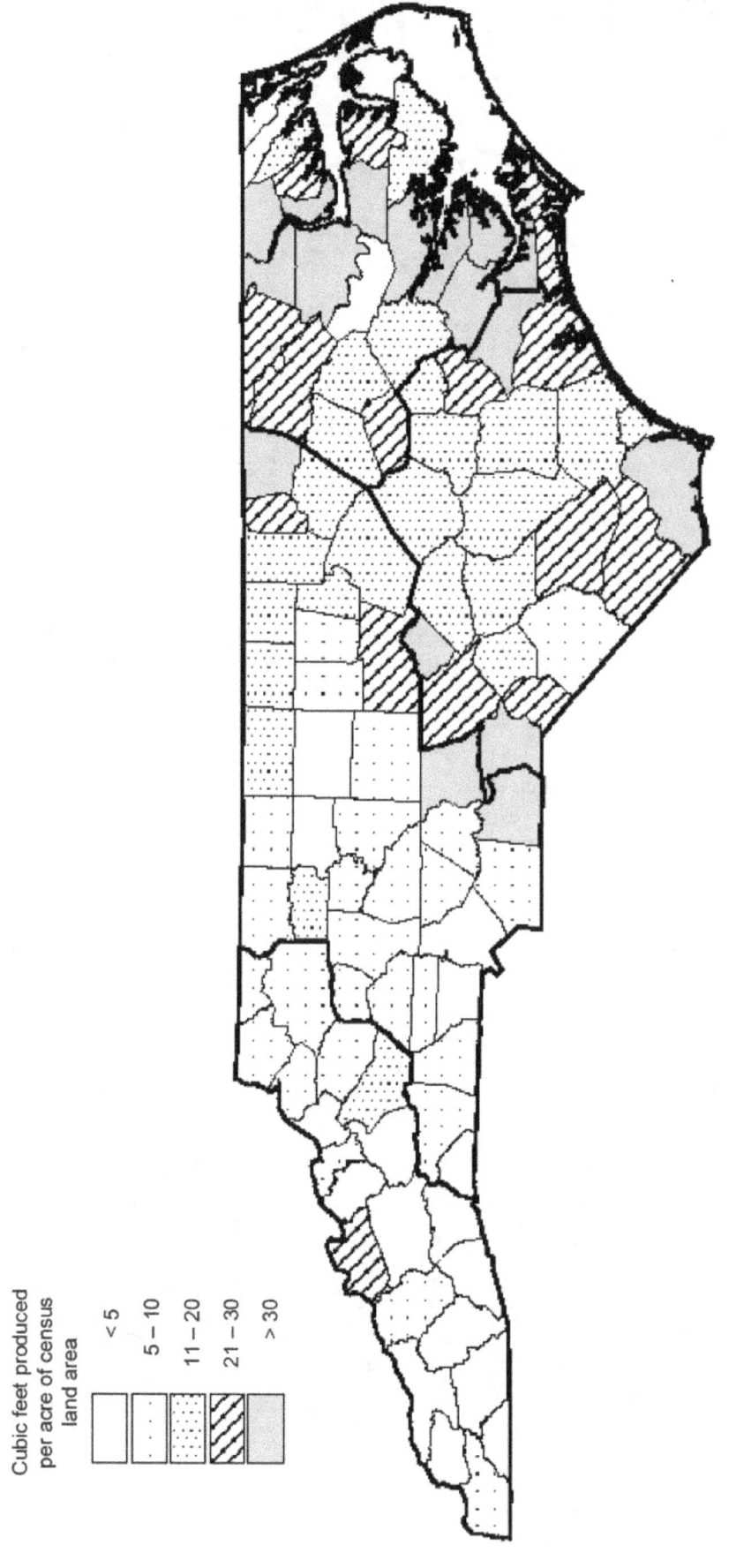

Cubic feet produced
per acre of census
land area

< 5

5 – 10

11 – 20

21 – 30

> 30

Figure 3—Intensity of roundwood softwood output for all industrial products in North Carolina by county, 2001.

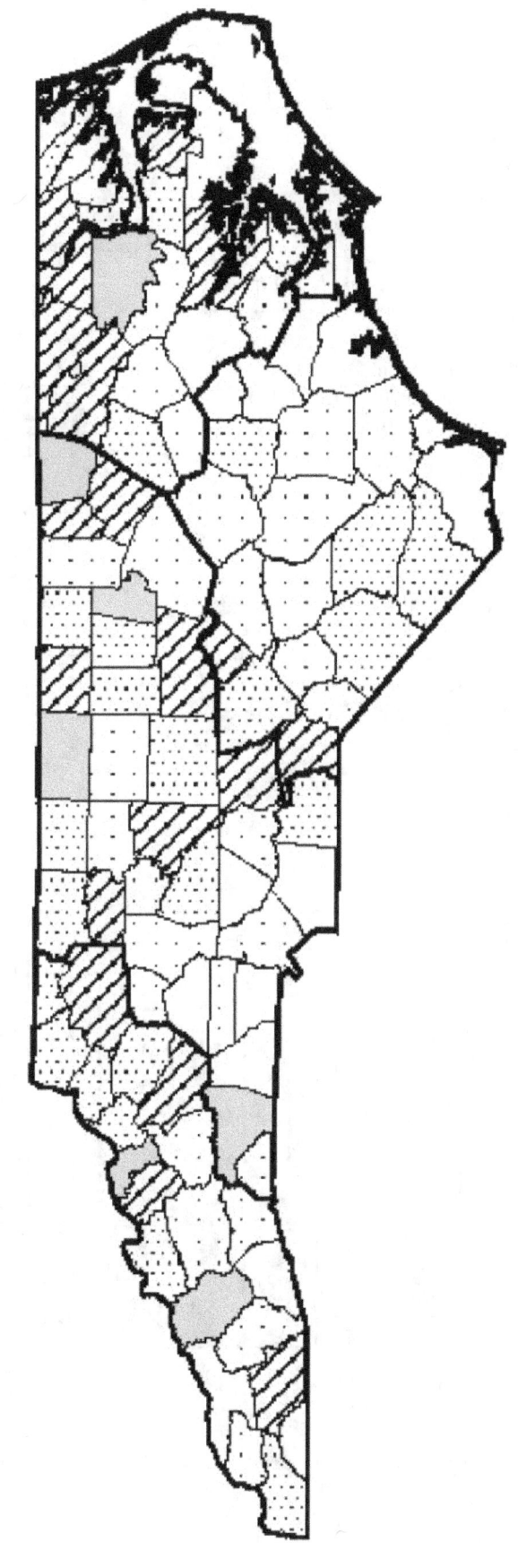

Cubic feet produced
per acre of census
land area

< 3

3 – 5

6 – 10

11 – 15

> 15

Figure 4—Intensity of roundwood hardwood output for all industrial products in North Carolina by county, 2001.

3

- Saw logs and pulpwood were the principal roundwood products in 2001. Combined output of these products totaled 668 million cubic feet and accounted for 88 percent of the State's total roundwood output (fig. 5).

- Total receipts at North Carolina mills, which included roundwood harvested and retained in the State as well as roundwood imported from other States, was down 47.5 million cubic feet to 722 million cubic feet. At the same time, the number of primary roundwood-using plants in North Carolina was down from 278 in 1999 to 249 in 2001.

**Saw Logs**

- Saw logs accounted for 56 percent of the State's total roundwood products. Output of softwood saw logs was up 4 percent to 309 million cubic feet (1.71 billion board feet, International ¼-inch rule), while output of hardwood saw logs declined 7 percent to 117 million cubic feet (704 million board feet, International ¼-inch rule) (fig. 6).

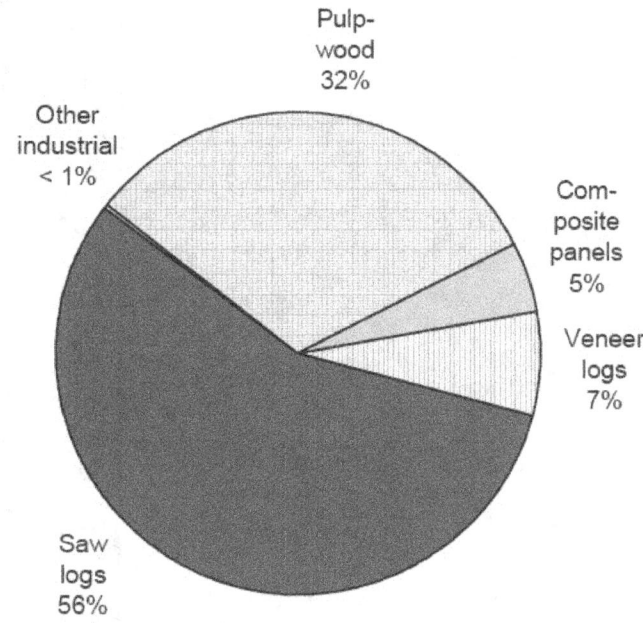

Total 759 million cubic feet

Figure 5—Roundwood production by type of product, 2001.

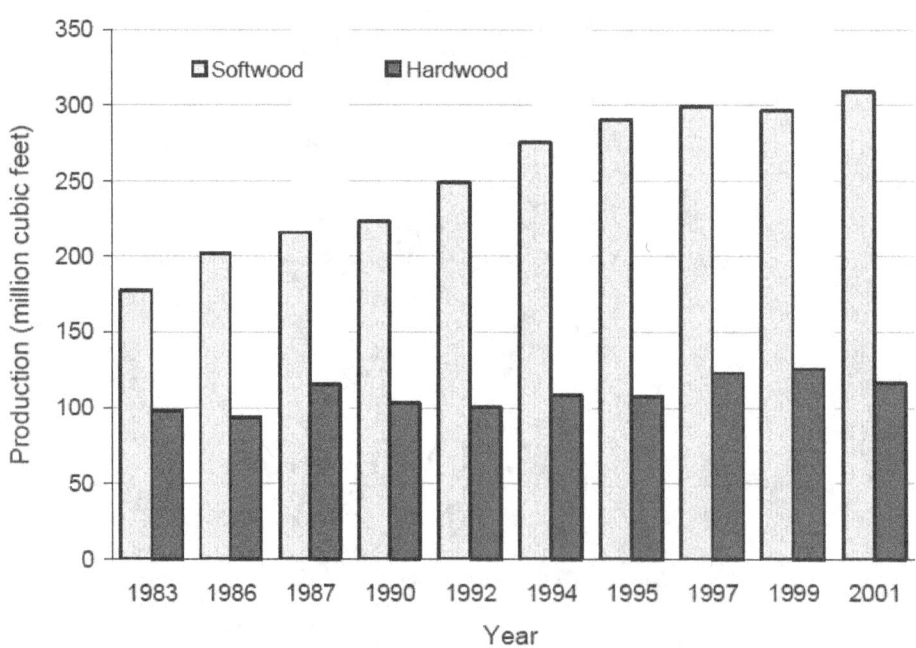

Figure 6—Roundwood pulpwood production by species group and year (see page 11 for references for individual years).

- In 2001, North Carolina had 215 sawmills, a net loss of 25 mills since 1999. Total saw-log receipts were up 5 million cubic feet to 430 million cubic feet. Softwood saw-log receipts were up 6 percent to 307 million cubic feet, while hardwood receipts declined 9 percent to 123 million cubic feet. Of the mills operating in 2001, 28 percent had receipts less than 1 million board feet, while 26 percent had receipts greater than 10 million board feet. Those 56 mills accounted for 83 percent of saw-log receipts.

- North Carolina retained 92 percent of its saw-log production for domestic manufacture, and saw-log imports exceeded exports by 4 million cubic feet in 2001.

## Pulpwood

- Pulpwood production, including chipped roundwood, declined 29 million cubic feet to 243 million cubic feet (3.3 million cords) and accounted for 32 percent of the State's total roundwood TPO. Softwood output was down 14 percent to 142 million cubic feet, while hardwood output declined 5 percent to 101 million cubic feet (fig. 7).

- Seven pulpmill facilities were operating and receiving roundwood in North Carolina in 2001, the same as in 1999. Total pulpwood receipts for these mills were down 53 million cubic feet to 191 million cubic feet, accounting for 27 percent of total receipts for all mills.

- Sixty-four percent of roundwood cut for pulpwood was retained for processing by North Carolina pulpmills. Roundwood pulpwood accounted for 66 percent of total known exports and 38 percent of total imports. Roundwood pulpwood exports amounted to 89 million cubic feet, while imports totaled 37 million cubic feet.

## Veneer Logs

- Output of veneer logs in 2001 totaled 53 million cubic feet and accounted for 7 percent of the State's total roundwood TPO volume. Softwood veneer production was down 18 percent to 34 million cubic feet (196 million board feet, International ¼-inch rule), while output of hardwood veneer logs remained unchanged at 19 million cubic feet (122 million board feet, International ¼-inch rule) (fig. 8).

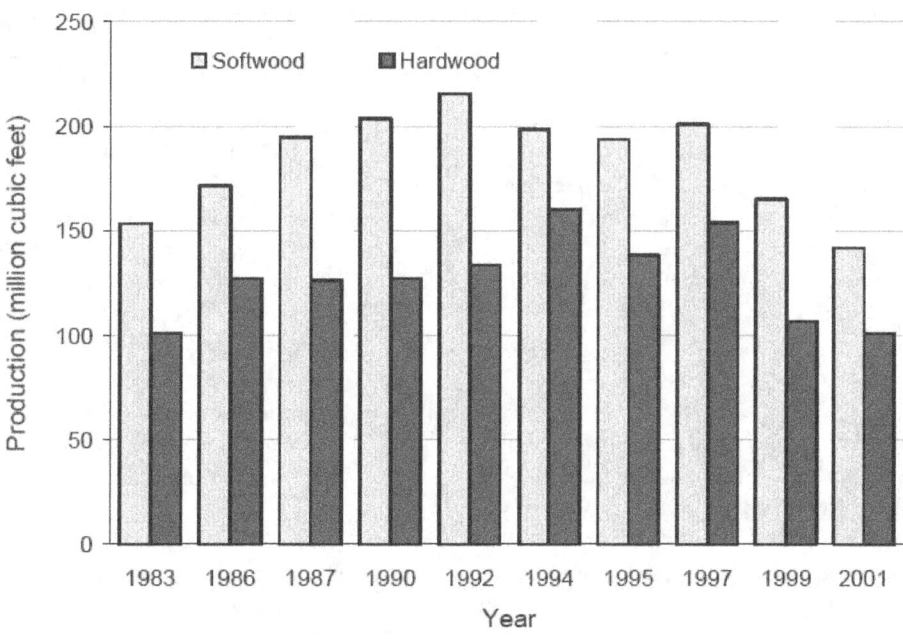

Figure 7—Roundwood saw-log production by species group and year (see page 11 for references for individual years).

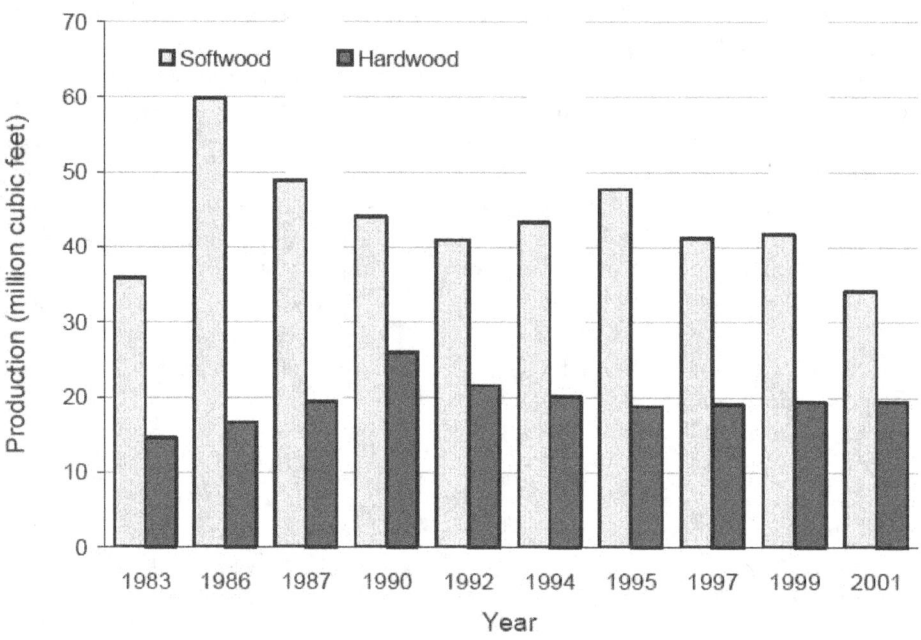

Figure 8—Roundwood veneer-log production by species group and year (see page 11 for references for individual years).

- The number of veneer mills operating in North Carolina declined from 24 in 1999 to 20 in 2001. Receipts of veneer logs declined 8 percent to 57 million cubic feet. Softwood veneer receipts were down 6.6 million cubic feet to 32 million cubic feet. Hardwood veneer receipts increased 8 percent to 25 million cubic feet.

- North Carolina retained 89 percent of its veneer-log production for processing at domestic veneer mills. Imports amounted to 9.0 million cubic feet, while exports totaled 5.6 million cubic feet, making the State a net importer of roundwood veneer logs.

**Composite Panels**

- Roundwood harvested from North Carolina's forests for composite panels declined 1 percent and totaled 36 million cubic feet (487 thousand cords). Softwood output declined 3 percent to 27 million cubic feet, while hardwood output was up 4 percent to 9 million cubic feet (fig. 9).

- Three composite panel mills were operating in North Carolina in 2001, the same as in 1999. Total receipts for these mills increased 15 percent to 43 million cubic feet.

- Eighty-eight percent of the composite panel production was retained for processing by North Carolina mills. Imports amounted to 11.1 million cubic feet, while exports totaled 4.2 million cubic feet, making the State a net importer of roundwood used for composite panels.

**Other Industrial Products**

- Roundwood harvested for other industrial uses, e.g., poles, posts, mulch, firewood, logs for log homes, and all other industrial products, totaled 1.0 million cubic feet, down 42 percent from 1999. Softwood made up 98 percent of the other industrial products volume.

- The number of plants producing other industrial products was four in 2001, the same as in 1999. Receipts of other industrial products totaled 893 thousand cubic feet.

- North Carolina was a net exporter of roundwood used for other industrial products; of the 180 thousand cubic feet exported, 88 percent was softwood whereas 100 percent of imports were softwood.

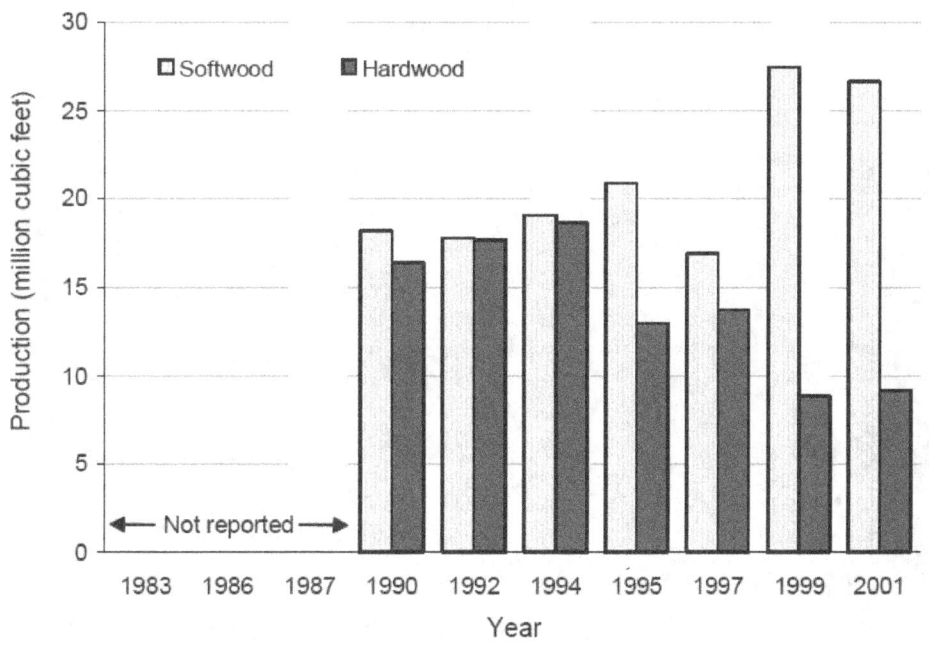

Figure 9—Roundwood production for composite panels by species group and year (see page 11 for references for individual years).

## Plant Byproducts

- In 2001, processing of primary products in North Carolina mills generated 313 million cubic feet of wood and bark residues. Coarse residues from all primary products amounted to 131 million cubic feet, while bark volume totaled 67 million cubic feet. Sawdust and shavings made up 37 percent of total residues, or 117 million cubic feet (fig. 10).

- Less than 1 percent of the wood and bark residues were not used for a product, while 36 percent of the residues were used for industrial fuel (fig. 11). More than 117 million cubic feet, or 90 percent, of the coarse residues were used to manufacture fiber products. Most of the bark was used for industrial fuel or other miscellaneous products, while 79 percent of the sawdust and 2 percent of the shavings were used for industrial fuel. Shavings were used primarily for particleboard manufacture or miscellaneous uses such as bedding.

- The processing of saw logs by sawmills generated 258 million cubic feet of mill residues, or 82 percent of the total residues produced (fig. 12).

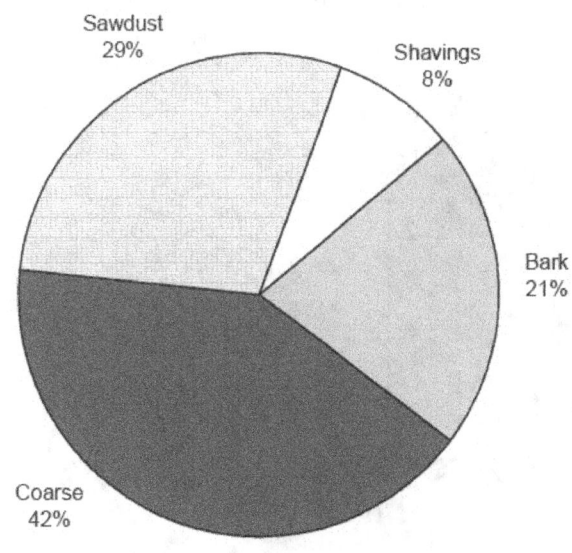

Total 314 million cubic feet

Figure 10—Primary mill residue by residue type, 2001.

7

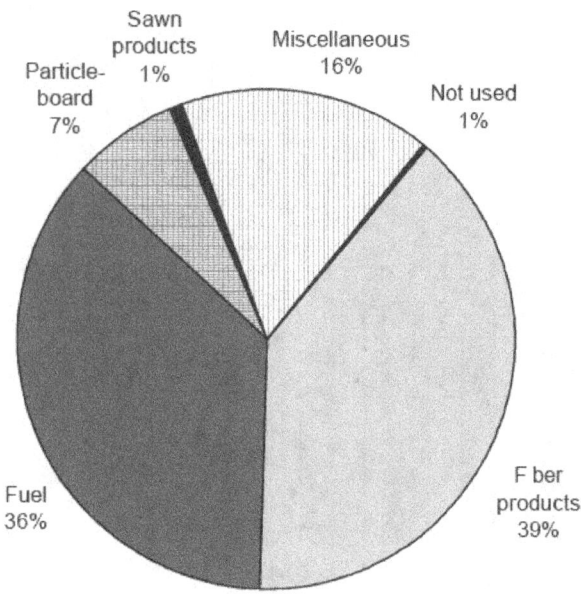

Total 314 million cubic feet

Figure 11—Disposal of residue by product, 2001.

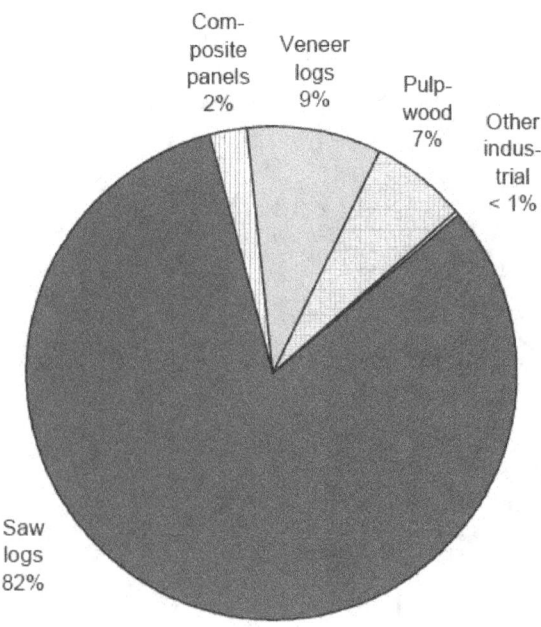

Total 314 million cubic feet

Figure 12—Primary mill residue produced by roundwood type, 2001.

## Regional Trends

- Output of industrial roundwood products declined in all regions, with the exception of the Northern Coastal Plain region of North Carolina. This region showed a 6-percent increase in product output. The Southern Coastal Plain and Piedmont regions had declines of 12 and 7 percent, respectively. The Mountain region had the smallest decline at less than 1 percent (fig. 13).

### Southern Coastal Plain Region

- Roundwood output from the Southern Coastal Plain region totaled 228 million cubic feet, down 12 percent. Softwood output declined 9 percent to 179 million cubic feet, while hardwood output was down 19 percent to 49 million cubic feet.

- Saw-log production of 107 million cubic feet accounted for 47 percent of the total roundwood output for the region. Pulpwood production of 83 million cubic feet accounted for 37 percent of the region's TPO and 34 percent of the State's roundwood pulpwood output.

- In the Southern Coastal Plain region, 35 primary wood-using plants were operating during 2001: 28 sawmills, 5 veneer or plywood mills, 1 pulpmill, and 1 composite panel mill. These mills processed 30 percent of the State's total roundwood output.

### Northern Coastal Plain Region

- The Northern Coastal Plain region had a 6-percent increase in roundwood output. Production was up from 219 million cubic feet in 1999 to 232 million cubic feet in 2001.

- Saw-log production of 129 million cubic feet accounted for 55 percent of the region's total roundwood output and 30 percent of the State's total saw-log output. Production of pulpwood was up 2 percent to 90 million cubic feet, but still accounted for 39 percent of the region's total roundwood output and 37 percent of the State's total roundwood pulpwood output.

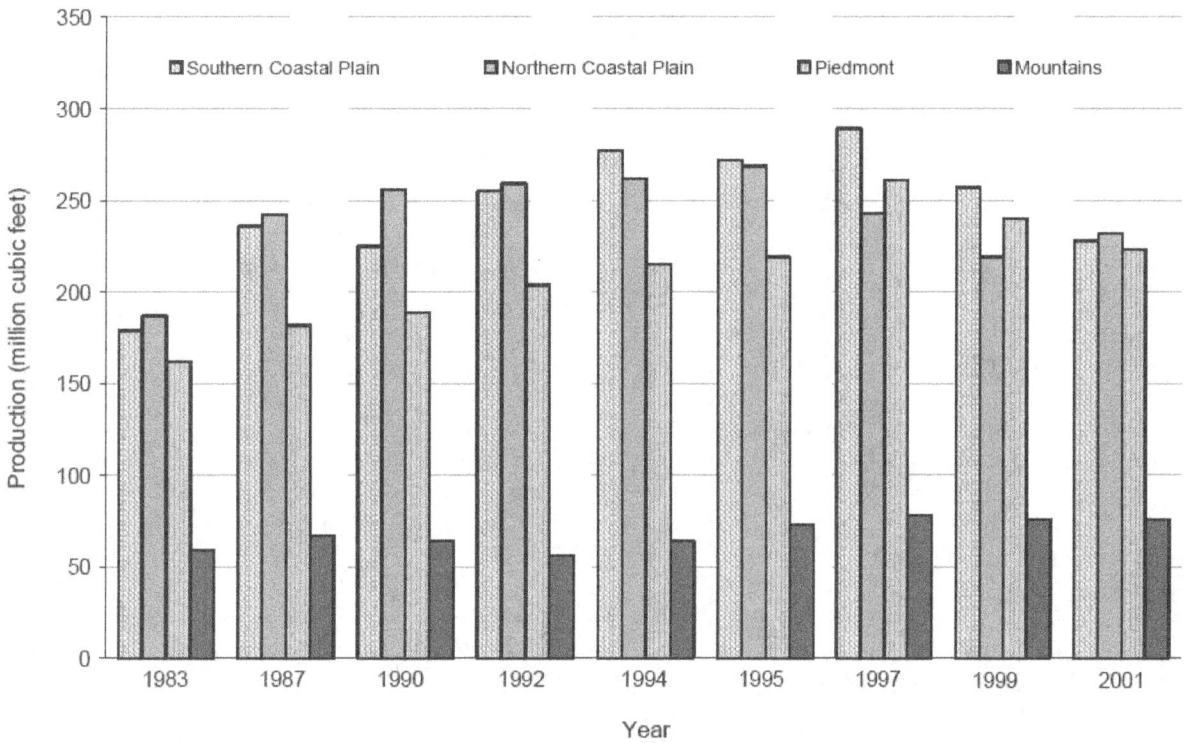

Figure 13—Roundwood production for all products by survey region and year (see page 11 for references for individual years).

- The 37 mills operating in the Northern Coastal Plain region in 2001 included 30 sawmills, 3 veneer or plywood mills, and 4 pulpmills. These mills processed 31 percent of the State's total roundwood output.

## Piedmont Region

- Roundwood output from the Piedmont region of North Carolina totaled 223 million cubic feet, a decline of 7 percent. Roundwood production from this region accounted for 29 percent of the total roundwood TPO for the State.

- Saw-log production of 139 million cubic feet accounted for 62 percent of the region's total roundwood output. Pulpwood production declined by 20 percent to 50 million cubic feet, accounting for 22 percent of the region's total TPO.

- The 105 primary wood-using plants operating in the Piedmont region included 91 sawmills, 8 veneer or plywood mills, 2 composite panel mills, and 4 other miscellaneous mills.

## Mountain Region

- Roundwood output from the Mountain region remained relatively stable at 76 million cubic feet.

- Saw-log production declined 3 percent to 50 million cubic feet and accounted for 66 percent of the region's total roundwood output. Pulpwood production was up 1 million cubic feet to 20 million cubic feet and accounted for 26 percent of the region's total TPO.

- In the Mountain region, 72 primary wood-using plants were operating during 2001: 66 sawmills, 4 veneer or plywood mills, and 2 pulpmills.

## Total Roundwood Output

Using the most recent inventory data for North Carolina, product output by source, ownership, and detailed species group was estimated.

### Source

- In addition to the 758 million cubic feet of industrial roundwood output, an estimated 90 million cubic feet was harvested for domestic fuelwood, bringing North Carolina's total roundwood output to 848 million cubic feet.

- Ninety-seven percent of total roundwood output was considered growing-stock volume (sawtimber and poletimber) from timberland sources. Other sources (such as saplings; stumps, tops, and limbs of trees on timberland; and trees on nonforest land) contributed an estimated 28 million cubic feet, or 3 percent of total roundwood output (fig. 14).

### Ownership

- An estimated 685 million cubic feet, or 81 percent, of the total roundwood output came from nonindustrial private forest lands. Forest industry lands contributed 136 million cubic feet, or 16 percent of the output. Public lands made up the remaining 3 percent, or 27 million cubic feet (fig. 15).

### Species

- The loblolly and shortleaf pine group provided the most volume of any softwood species group; at 411 million cubic feet, it accounted for 79 percent of the total softwood output (fig. 16). Other yellow pine types accounted for another 11 percent of softwood output. The red oak and white oak groups combined accounted for 115 million cubic feet, or 35 percent of total hardwood output (fig. 17).

Poletimber
25%

Other
3%

Sawtimber
72%

Total 848 million cubic feet

Figure 14—Roundwood output by source, 2001.

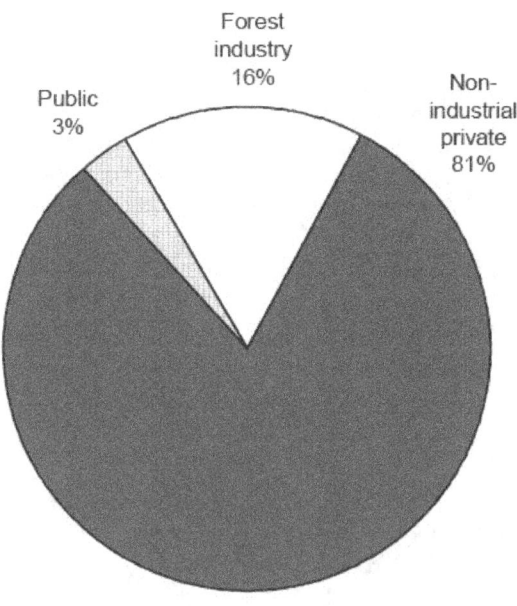

Forest
industry
16%

Public
3%

Non-
industrial
private
81%

Total 848 million cubic feet

Figure 15—Roundwood output by ownership, 2001.

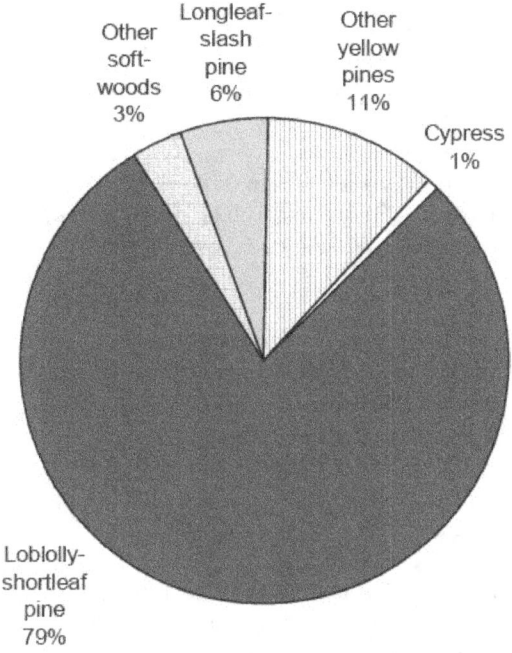

Total 522 million cubic feet

Figure 16—Roundwood output by softwood species group, 2001.

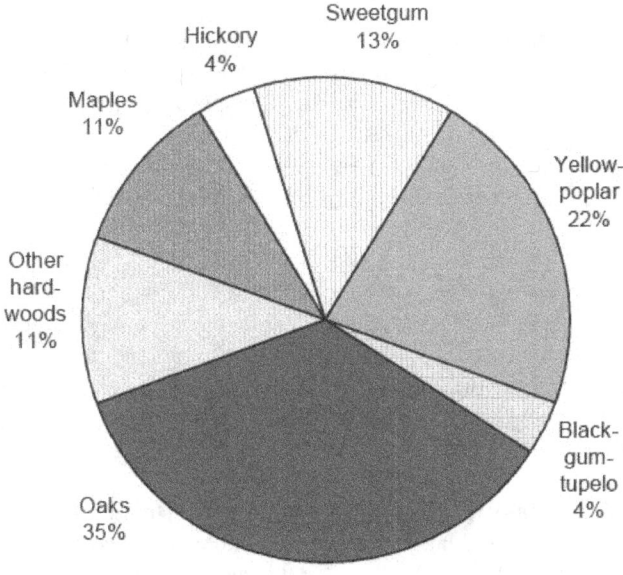

Total 327 million cubic feet

Figure 17—Roundwood output by hardwood species group, 2001.

## References

Davenport, Edgar L. 1992. Changes in North Carolina's industrial roundwood products output, 1987-1990. Resour. Bull. SE-132. Asheville, NC: U.S. Department of Agriculture, Forest Service, Southeastern Forest Experiment Station. 22 p. [1987, 1990].

Hutchins, Cecil C., Jr. 1983. Changes in output of industrial timber products in North Carolina, 1973-1979. Resour. Bull. SE-70. Asheville, NC: U.S. Department of Agriculture, Forest Service, Southeastern Forest Experiment Station. 23 p. [1979].

Johnson, Tony G. 1994. North Carolina's timber industry—an assessment of timber product output and use, 1992. Resour. Bull. SE-146. Asheville, NC: U.S. Department of Agriculture, Forest Service, Southeastern Forest Experiment Station. 30 p. [1992].

Johnson, Tony G.; Brown, David R. 1996. North Carolina's timber industry—an assessment of timber product output and use, 1994. Resour. Bull. SRS-4. Asheville, NC: U.S. Department of Agriculture, Forest Service, Southern Research Station. 31 p. [1994].

Johnson, Tony G.; Brown, David R. 1999. North Carolina's timber industry—an assessment of timber product output and use, 1997. Resour. Bull. SRS-39. Asheville, NC: U.S. Department of Agriculture, Forest Service, Southern Research Station. 34 p. [1997].

Johnson, Tony G.; Brown, David R. 2002. North Carolina's timber industry—an assessment of timber product output and use, 1999. Resour. Bull. SRS-73. Asheville, NC: U.S. Department of Agriculture, Forest Service, Southern Research Station. 39 p. [1997].

Johnson, Tony G.; Jenkins, Anne; Brown, David R. 1997. North Carolina's timber industry—an assessment of timber product output and use, 1995. Resour. Bull. SRS-18. Asheville, NC: U.S. Department of Agriculture, Forest Service, Southern Research Station. 35 p. [1995].

U.S. Department of Agriculture, Forest Service. Product drain by county, product, and species. 6 p. Unpublished data. On file with: Southern Research Station, Forest Inventory and Analysis Research Work Unit, 4700 Old Kingston Pike, Knoxville, TN 37919. [1983, 1986].

## Definition of Terms

**Board foot.** A unit of measure applied to lumber that is 1-foot long, 1-foot wide, and 1-inch thick (or its equivalent) and also associated with roundwood as to its potential yield of such products.

**Byproducts.** Primary wood products, e.g., pulp chips, animal bedding, and fuelwood, recycled from mill residues.

**Composite panels.** Roundwood products manufactured into chips, wafers, strands, flakes, shavings, or sawdust and then reconstituted into a variety of panel and engineered lumber products.

**Consumption.** The quantity of a commodity, such as pulpwood, utilized by a particular mill or group of mills.

**Drain.** The volume of roundwood removed from any geographic area where timber is grown.

**Exports.** The volume of domestic roundwood utilized by mills outside the State where timber was cut.

**Fiber products.** Byproducts used in the manufacture of pulp, paper, paperboard, and composite products, such as chipboard.

**Fuelwood production.** The volume of roundwood harvested to produce some form of energy, e.g., heat, steam, in residential, industrial, or institutional settings.

**Growing-stock removals.** The growing-stock volume removed from poletimber and sawtimber trees in the timber-land inventory. (Note: Includes volume removed for round-wood products, logging residues, and other removals.)

**Growing-stock trees.** Living trees of commercial species classified as sawtimber, poletimber, saplings, and seedlings. Growing-stock trees must contain at least one 12-foot or two 8-foot logs in the saw-log portion, currently or potentially (if too small to qualify). The log(s) must meet dimension and merchantability standards and have, currently or potentially, one-third of the gross board-foot volume in sound wood.

**Growing-stock volume.** The cubic-foot volume of sound wood in growing-stock trees at least 5.0 inches d.b.h. from a 1-foot stump to a minimum 4.0-inch top d.o.b. of the central stem.

**Hardwoods.** Dicotyledonous trees, usually broadleaf and deciduous.

*Soft hardwoods.* Hardwood species with an average specific gravity of 0.50 or less, such as gums, yellow-poplar, cottonwoods, red maple, basswoods, and willows.

*Hard hardwoods.* Hardwood species with an average specific gravity greater than 0.50, such as oaks, hard maples, hickories, and beech.

**Imports.** The volume of domestic roundwood delivered to a mill or group of mills in a specific State but harvested outside that State.

**Industrial fuelwood.** A roundwood product, with or without bark, used to generate energy at a manufacturing facility such as a wood-using mill.

**Industrial roundwood products.** Any primary use of the main stem of a tree, such as saw logs, pulpwood, veneer logs, intended to be processed into primary wood products such as lumber, wood pulp, sheathing, at primary wood-using mills.

**International ¼-inch rule.** A log rule or formula for estimating the board-foot volume of logs, allowing ½-inch of taper for each 4-foot length. The rule appears in a number of forms that allow for kerf. In the form used by FIA, a ¼-inch of kerf is assumed. This rule is used as the USDA Forest Service standard log rule in the Eastern United States.

**Log.** A primary forest product harvested in long, primarily 8-, 12-, and 16-foot lengths.

**Logging residues.** The unused merchantable portion of growing-stock trees cut or destroyed during logging operations.

**Merchantable portion.** That portion of live trees 5.0 inches d.b.h. and larger between a 1-foot stump and a minimum 4.0-inch top d.o.b. on the central stem. That portion of primary forks from the point of occurrence to a minimum 4.0-inch top d.o.b. is included.

**Merchantable volume.** Solid-wood volume in the merchantable portion of live trees.

**Noncommercial species.** Tree species of typically small size, poor form, or inferior quality that normally do not develop into trees suitable for industrial wood products.

**Nonforest land.** Land that has never supported forests and land formerly forested where timber production is precluded by development for other uses.

**Nongrowing-stock sources.** The net volume removed from the nongrowing-stock portions of poletimber and sawtimber trees (stumps, tops, limbs, cull sections of central stem) and from any portion of a rough, rotten, sapling, dead, or nonforest tree.

**Other forest land.** Forest land other than timberland and productive reserved forest land. It includes available and reserved forest land that is incapable of producing annually 20 cubic feet per acre of industrial wood under natural conditions because of adverse site conditions such as sterile soils, dry climate, poor drainage, high elevation, steepness, or rockiness.

**Other products.** A miscellaneous category of roundwood products, e.g., cooperage, excelsior, shingles, and mill residue byproducts (charcoal, bedding, mulch, etc.).

**Other removals.** The growing-stock volume of trees removed from the inventory by cultural operations such as timber stand improvement, land clearing, and other changes in land use, resulting in the removal of the trees from timberland.

**Other sources.** (See: Nongrowing-stock sources.)

**Ownership.** The property owned by one ownership unit, including all parcels of land in the United States.

*National forest land.* Federal land that has been legally designated as national forests or purchase units, and other land under the administration of the Forest Service, including experimental areas and Bankhead-Jones Title III land.

*Forest industry land.* Land owned by companies or individuals operating primary wood-using plants.

*Nonindustrial private forest (NIPF) land.* Privately owned land excluding forest industry land.

Corporate. Owned by corporations, including incorporated farm ownerships.

Individual. All lands owned by individuals, including farm operators.

*Other public.* An ownership class that includes all public lands except national forests.

Miscellaneous Federal land. Federal land other than national forests.

State, county, and municipal land. Land owned by States, counties, and local public agencies or municipalities, or land leased to these governmental units for 50 years or more.

**Plant residues.** Wood material generated in the production of timber products at primary manufacturing plants.

*Coarse residues.* Material, such as slabs, edgings, trim, veneer cores and ends, which is suitable for chipping.

*Fine residues.* Material, such as sawdust, shavings, and veneer residue, which is not suitable for chipping.

*Plant byproducts.* Residues (coarse or fine) used in the further manufacture of industrial products for consumer use or as fuel.

*Unused plant residues.* Residues (coarse or fine) that are not used for any product, including fuel.

**Posts, poles, and pilings.** Roundwood products milled (cut or peeled) into standard sizes (lengths and circumferences) to be put in the ground to provide vertical and lateral support in buildings, foundations, utility lines, and fences. May also include nonindustrial (unmilled) products.

**Poletimber-size trees.** Softwoods 5.0 to 8.9 inches d.b.h. and hardwoods 5.0 to 10.9 inches d.b.h.

**Primary wood-using plants.** Industries that convert roundwood products (saw logs, veneer logs, pulpwood, etc.) into primary wood products, such as lumber, veneer or sheathing, wood pulp.

**Production.** The total volume of known roundwood harvested from land within a State, regardless of where it is consumed. Production is the sum of timber harvested and used within a State, and all roundwood exported to other States.

**Pulpwood.** A roundwood product that will be reduced to individual wood fibers by chemical or mechanical means. The fibers are used to make a broad generic group of pulp products that includes paper products, as well as fiberboard, insulating board, and paperboard.

**Receipts.** The quantity or volume of industrial roundwood received at a mill or by a group of mills in a State, regardless of the geographic source. Volume of roundwood receipts is equal to the volume of roundwood retained in a State plus roundwood imported from other States.

**Retained.** Roundwood volume harvested from and processed by mills within the same State.

**Rotten trees.** Live trees of commercial species not containing at least one 12-foot saw log, or two noncontiguous saw logs, each 8 feet or longer, now or prospectively, primarily because of rot or missing sections, and with less than one-third of the gross board-foot tree volume in sound material.

**Rough trees.** Live trees of commercial species not containing at least one 12-foot saw log, or two noncontiguous saw logs, each 8 feet or longer, now or prospectively, primarily because of roughness, poor form, splits, and cracks, and with less than one-third of the gross broad-foot tree volume in sound material; and live trees of noncommercial species.

**Roundwood (roundwood logs).** Logs, bolts, or other round sections cut from trees for industrial manufacture or consumer uses.

**Roundwood chipped.** Any timber cut primarily for industrial manufacture, delivered to nonpulpmills, chipped, and then sold to pulpmills for use as fiber. Includes tops, jump sections, whole trees, and pulpwood sticks.

**Roundwood products.** Any primary product, such as lumber, veneer, composite panels, poles, pilings, pulp, or fuelwood that is produced from roundwood.

**Roundwood product drain.** That portion of total drain used for a product.

**Salvable dead trees.** Standing or downed dead trees that were formerly growing stock and considered merchantable. Trees must be at least 5.0 inches d.b.h. to qualify.

**Saplings.** Live trees 1.0 to 5.0 inches d.b.h.

**Saw log.** A roundwood product, usually 8 feet in length or longer, processed into a variety of sawn products such as lumber, cants, pallets, railroad ties, and timbers.

**Saw-log portion.** The part of the bole of sawtimber trees between a 1-foot stump and the saw-log top.

**Saw-log top.** The point on the bole of sawtimber trees above which a conventional saw log cannot be produced. The minimum saw-log top is 7.0 inches d.o.b. for softwoods and 9.0 inches d.o.b. for hardwoods for FIA standards.

**Sawtimber-size trees.** Softwoods 9.0 inches d.b.h. and larger and hardwoods 11.0 inches d.b.h. and larger.

**Sawtimber volume.** Growing-stock volume in the saw-log portion of sawtimber-sized trees in board feet (International ¼-inch rule).

**Seedlings.** Trees less than 1.0 inch d.b.h. and greater than 1 foot tall for hardwoods, greater than 6 inches tall for softwood, and greater than 0.5 inch in diameter at ground level for longleaf pine.

**Select red oaks.** A group of several red oak species composed of cherrybark, Shumard, and northern red oaks. Other red oak species are included in the "other red oaks" group.

**Select white oaks.** A group of several white oak species composed of white, swamp chestnut, swamp white, chinkapin, Durand, and bur oaks. Other white oak species are included in the "other white oaks" group.

**Softwoods.** Coniferous trees, usually evergreen, having leaves that are needles or scalelike.

**Standard cord.** A unit of measure applied to roundwood, usually bolts or split wood. It is a stack of wood 4 feet high, 4 feet wide, and 8 feet long encompassing 128 cubic feet of wood, bark, and air space. This usually translates to approximately 75.0 to 81.0 cubic feet of solid wood for pulpwood, because pulpwood is more uniform.

**Standard unit.** A unit measure applied to roundwood timber products. Board feet (International ¼-inch rule) is the standard unit used for saw logs and veneer; cords are used for pulpwood, composite panel, and fuelwood; hundred pieces for poles; thousand pieces for posts; and thousand cubic feet for all other miscellaneous forest products.

**Timberland.** Forest land capable of producing 20 cubic feet of industrial wood per acre per year and not withdrawn from timber utilization.

**Timber products.** Roundwood products and byproducts.

**Timber products output.** The total volume of roundwood products from all sources plus the volume of byproducts recovered from mill residues (equals roundwood product drain).

**Timber removals.** The total volume of trees removed from the timberland inventory by harvesting, cultural operations such as stand improvement, land clearing, or changes in land use. (Note: Includes roundwood products, logging residues, and other removals.)

**Tree.** Woody plants having one erect perennial stem or trunk at least 3 inches d.b.h., a more or less definitely formed crown of foliage, and a height of at least 13 feet (at maturity).

**Upper-stem portion.** The part of the main stem of sawtimber trees above the saw-log top and the minimum top diameter of 4.0 inches outside bark, or to the point where the main stem breaks into limbs.

**Utilization studies.** Studies conducted on active logging operations to develop factors for merchantable portions of trees left in the woods (logging residues), logging damage, and utilization of the unmerchantable portion of growing-stock trees and nongrowing-stock trees.

**Veneer log.** A roundwood product either rotary cut, sliced, stamped, or sawn into a variety of veneer products such as plywood, finished panels, veneer sheets, or sheathing.

**Weight.** A unit of measure for mill residues, expressed as oven-dry tons (2,000 oven-dry pounds).

## Conversion Factors[a]

**Saw logs**

| | |
|---|---|
| Softwood | 0.18018 cubic foot = 1 board foot |
| | 5.55 board feet = 1 cubic foot |
| Hardwood | 0.16556 cubic foot = 1 board foot |
| | 6.04 board feet = 1 cubic foot |

**Veneer logs**

| | |
|---|---|
| Softwood | 0.17391 cubic foot = 1 board foot |
| | 5.75 board feet = 1 cubic foot |
| Hardwood | 0.15873 cubic foot = 1 board foot |
| | 6.30 board feet = 1 cubic foot |

**Pulpwood[b]**

| | |
|---|---|
| Softwood | 72.5 cubic feet per cord |
| Hardwood | 76.6 cubic feet per cord |

[a] Conversion factors vary with stem size (d.b.h.) and species. The factors shown are for trees of average diameters removed in North Carolina during the most recent survey period.

[b] Cubic feet of solid wood per cord.

## Index of Tables

**Table 1—Output of industrial products by product and species group, North Carolina, 1999 and 2001**

| Product and species group | Year 1999 | Year 2001 | Change | Percent change |
|---|---|---|---|---|
| | *thousand cubic feet* | | | |
| **Saw logs** | | | | |
| Softwood | 296,290 | 308,668 | 12,378 | 4.2 |
| Hardwood | 125,778 | 116,581 | -9,197 | -7.3 |
| Total | 422,068 | 425,249 | 3,181 | 0.8 |
| **Veneer logs** | | | | |
| Softwood | 41,748 | 34,117 | -7,631 | -18.3 |
| Hardwood | 19,310 | 19,302 | -8 | -- |
| Total | 61,058 | 53,419 | -7,639 | -12.5 |
| **Pulpwood**[a] | | | | |
| Softwood | 164,991 | 141,903 | -23,088 | -14.0 |
| Hardwood | 106,854 | 101,098 | -5,756 | -5.4 |
| Total | 271,845 | 243,001 | -28,844 | -10.6 |
| **Composite panels** | | | | |
| Softwood | 27,450 | 26,610 | -840 | -3.1 |
| Hardwood | 8,860 | 9,184 | 324 | 3.7 |
| Total | 36,310 | 35,794 | -516 | -1.4 |
| **Other industrial** | | | | |
| Softwood | 1,778 | 1,015 | -763 | -42.9 |
| Hardwood | 0 | 22 | 22 | -- |
| Total | 1,778 | 1,037 | -741 | -41.7 |
| **All industrial** | | | | |
| Softwood | 532,257 | 512,313 | -19,944 | -3.7 |
| Hardwood | 260,802 | 246,187 | -14,615 | -5.6 |
| Total | 793,059 | 758,500 | -34,559 | -4.4 |
| **Byproduct output** | | | | |
| Softwood | 207,323 | 215,722 | 8,399 | 4.1 |
| Hardwood | 103,597 | 97,757 | -5,840 | -5.6 |
| Total | 310,920 | 313,479 | 2,559 | 0.8 |
| **Total output** | | | | |
| Softwood | 739,580 | 728,035 | -11,545 | -1.6 |
| Hardwood | 364,399 | 343,944 | -20,455 | -5.6 |
| Total | 1,103,979 | 1,071,979 | -32,000 | -2.9 |

-- = negligible.

[a] Includes roundwood delivered to nonpulpmills, then chipped and sold to pulpmills (7,369,000 cubic feet in 1999 and 7,746,000 cubic feet in 2001).

**Table 2—Roundwood receipts by product and species group, North Carolina, 1999 and 2001**

| Product and species group | Year | | Change | Percent change |
|---|---|---|---|---|
| | 1999 | 2001 | | |
| | *thousand cubic feet* | | | |
| **Saw logs** | | | | |
| Softwood | 289,528 | 306,583 | 17,055 | 5.9 |
| Hardwood | 135,271 | 123,161 | -12,110 | -9.0 |
| Total | 424,799 | 429,744 | 4,945 | 1.2 |
| **Veneer logs** | | | | |
| Softwood | 38,652 | 32,079 | -6,573 | -17.0 |
| Hardwood | 22,973 | 24,688 | 1,715 | 7.5 |
| Total | 61,625 | 56,767 | -4,858 | -7.9 |
| **Pulpwood**[a] | | | | |
| Softwood | 144,808 | 122,656 | -22,152 | -15.3 |
| Hardwood | 99,480 | 68,824 | -30,656 | -30.8 |
| Total | 244,288 | 191,480 | -52,808 | -21.6 |
| **Composite panels** | | | | |
| Softwood | 26,136 | 30,387 | 4,251 | 16.3 |
| Hardwood | 10,888 | 12,335 | 1,447 | 13.3 |
| Total | 37,024 | 42,722 | 5,698 | 15.4 |
| **Other industrial** | | | | |
| Softwood | 1,411 | 893 | -518 | -36.7 |
| Hardwood | 0 | 0 | 0 | -- |
| Total | 1,411 | 893 | -518 | -36.7 |
| **Total output** | | | | |
| Softwood | 500,535 | 492,598 | -7,937 | -1.6 |
| Hardwood | 268,612 | 229,008 | -39,604 | -14.7 |
| Total | 769,147 | 721,606 | -47,541 | -6.2 |

-- = negligible.

[a] Includes roundwood delivered to nonpulpmills, then chipped and sold to pulpmills (8,419,000 cubic feet in 1999 and 9,132,000 cubic feet in 2001).

Table 3—Number of primary wood-using plants by industry, North Carolina, 1983-2001

| Industry | Year | | | | | | | | | |
|---|---|---|---|---|---|---|---|---|---|---|
| | 1983 | 1986 | 1987 | 1990 | 1992 | 1994 | 1995 | 1997 | 1999 | 2001 |
| Sawmills | 429 | 336 | 362 | 308 | 306 | 275 | 273 | 243 | 240 | 215 |
| Veneer mills | 33 | 32 | 31 | 32 | 29 | 27 | 27 | 23 | 24 | 20 |
| Pulpmills | 8 | 8 | 8 | 8 | 8 | 8 | 8 | 7 | 7 | 7 |
| Composite panel mills | 0 | 4 | 4 | 5 | 4 | 4 | 4 | 3 | 3 | 3 |
| Other mills | 14 | 15 | 17 | 13 | 10 | 8 | 8 | 4 | 4 | 4 |
| All plants | 484 | 395 | 422 | 366 | 357 | 322 | 320 | 280 | 278 | 249 |

Table 4—Roundwood receipts by sawmill size, North Carolina, 1999 and 2001

| Sawmill size class[a] | 1999 | | | 2001 | | |
|---|---|---|---|---|---|---|
| | Number of mills | Thousand board feet | Percent of volume | Number of mills | Thousand board feet | Percent of volume |
| million board feet | | | | | | |
| <1.0 | 67 | 23,031 | 1 | 60 | 19,496 | 1 |
| 1.0–4.99 | 74 | 199,407 | 8 | 65 | 159,215 | 6 |
| 5.0–9.99 | 35 | 228,410 | 9 | 34 | 233,464 | 10 |
| 10.0–49.99 | 54 | 1,112,407 | 46 | 44 | 854,144 | 35 |
| >50 | 10 | 860,111 | 36 | 12 | 1,179,243 | 48 |
| Total | 240 | 2,423,366 | 100 | 215 | 2,445,562 | 100 |

[a] Based on volume received as opposed to actual capacity.

**Table 5—Roundwood receipts by species and type of mill, North Carolina, 2001**

| Species | All mills | Sawmills | Veneer mills Pine plywood | Veneer mills Other veneer | OSB[a] and panels | Pulpmills[b] | Other mills |
|---|---|---|---|---|---|---|---|
| | | | *thousand cubic feet* | | | | |
| **Softwood** | | | | | | | |
| Yellow pine | 349,464 | 286,913 | 31,797 | 278 | 29,583 | NA | 893 |
| Eastern white pine | 17,998 | 17,190 | 0 | 4 | 804 | NA | 0 |
| Cedar | 27 | 27 | 0 | 0 | 0 | NA | 0 |
| Cypress | 2,081 | 2,081 | 0 | 0 | 0 | NA | 0 |
| Other softwood | 372 | 372 | 0 | 0 | 0 | NA | 0 |
| Unclassified | 122,656 | 0 | 0 | 0 | 0 | 122,656 | 0 |
| Total softwoods | 492,598 | 306,583 | 31,797 | 282 | 30,387 | 122,656 | 893 |
| **Hardwood** | | | | | | | |
| Blackgum and tupelo | 6,151 | 3,957 | 855 | 318 | 1,021 | NA | 0 |
| Soft maple | 7,246 | 6,250 | 71 | 0 | 925 | NA | 0 |
| Sweetgum | 22,307 | 10,224 | 7,952 | 1,805 | 2,326 | NA | 0 |
| Yellow-poplar | 59,704 | 40,302 | 6,447 | 6,005 | 6,950 | NA | 0 |
| Other soft hardwood | 2,409 | 1,291 | 144 | 30 | 944 | NA | 0 |
| Hickory | 3,608 | 3,589 | 0 | 19 | 0 | NA | 0 |
| Red oak | 29,252 | 28,719 | 73 | 291 | 169 | NA | 0 |
| White oak | 21,960 | 21,708 | 0 | 252 | 0 | NA | 0 |
| Other hard hardwood | 7,547 | 7,121 | 0 | 426 | 0 | NA | 0 |
| Unclassified | 68,824 | 0 | 0 | 0 | 0 | 68,824 | 0 |
| Total hardwoods | 229,008 | 123,161 | 15,542 | 9,146 | 12,335 | 68,824 | 0 |
| **All species** | 721,606 | 429,744 | 47,339 | 9,428 | 42,722 | 191,480 | 893 |

NA = not applicable.

[a] OSB = oriented strand board.

[b] Collected only by softwood and hardwood and includes roundwood chipped.

**Table 6—Industrial roundwood movement by year and species group, North Carolina, 1999 and 2001**

| Year | Production | Exported to other States | Retained | Imported from other States | Receipts |
|---|---|---|---|---|---|
| | | *thousand cubic feet* | | | |
| | | **Softwood** | | | |
| 1999 | 532,257 | 86,107 | 446,150 | 54,385 | 500,535 |
| 2001 | 512,313 | 81,718 | 430,595 | 62,003 | 492,598 |
| | | **Hardwood** | | | |
| 1999 | 260,802 | 30,156 | 230,646 | 37,966 | 268,612 |
| 2001 | 246,187 | 51,514 | 194,673 | 34,335 | 229,008 |
| | | **All species** | | | |
| 1999 | 793,059 | 116,263 | 676,796 | 92,351 | 769,147 |
| 2001 | 758,500 | 133,232 | 625,268 | 96,338 | 721,606 |

Table 7—Industrial roundwood movement by product and species group, North Carolina, 2001

| Product and species group | Production | Exported to other States | Retained | Imported from other States | Receipts |
|---|---|---|---|---|---|
| | | | *thousand cubic feet* | | |
| **Saw logs** | | | | | |
| Softwood | 308,668 | 28,035 | 280,633 | 25,950 | 306,583 |
| Hardwood | 116,581 | 6,715 | 109,866 | 13,295 | 123,161 |
| Total | 425,249 | 34,750 | 390,499 | 39,245 | 429,744 |
| **Veneer logs** | | | | | |
| Softwood | 34,117 | 5,238 | 28,879 | 3,200 | 32,079 |
| Hardwood | 19,302 | 382 | 18,920 | 5,768 | 24,688 |
| Total | 53,419 | 5,620 | 47,799 | 8,968 | 56,767 |
| **Pulpwood**[a] | | | | | |
| Softwood | 141,903 | 44,447 | 97,456 | 25,200 | 122,656 |
| Hardwood | 101,098 | 44,068 | 57,030 | 11,794 | 68,824 |
| Total | 243,001 | 88,515 | 154,486 | 36,994 | 191,480 |
| **Composite panels** | | | | | |
| Softwood | 26,610 | 3,840 | 22,770 | 7,617 | 30,387 |
| Hardwood | 9,184 | 327 | 8,857 | 3,478 | 12,335 |
| Total | 35,794 | 4,167 | 31,627 | 11,095 | 42,722 |
| **Other industrial** | | | | | |
| Softwood | 1,015 | 158 | 857 | 36 | 893 |
| Hardwood | 22 | 22 | 0 | 0 | 0 |
| Total | 1,037 | 180 | 857 | 36 | 893 |
| **All products** | | | | | |
| Softwood | 512,313 | 81,718 | 430,595 | 62,003 | 492,598 |
| Hardwood | 246,187 | 51,514 | 194,673 | 34,335 | 229,008 |
| Total | 758,500 | 133,232 | 625,268 | 96,338 | 721,606 |

[a] Includes roundwood chipped.

**Table 8—Saw-log volume by destination, source, and species group, North Carolina, 2001**

| Destination and source | All species | Species group | |
| --- | --- | --- | --- |
| | | Softwood | Hardwood |
| | *thousand cubic feet* | | |
| **North Carolina (retained)** | 390,499 | 280,633 | 109,866 |
| **Exports to:** | | | |
| Florida | 132 | 102 | 30 |
| Georgia | 269 | 259 | 10 |
| South Carolina | 10,921 | 10,341 | 580 |
| Tennessee | 1,965 | 978 | 987 |
| Virginia | 21,463 | 16,355 | 5,108 |
| Total | 34,750 | 28,035 | 6,715 |
| **Imports from:** | | | |
| Florida | 37 | 37 | 0 |
| Georgia | 1,637 | 125 | 1,512 |
| South Carolina | 12,382 | 6,222 | 6,160 |
| Tennessee | 2,073 | 1,096 | 977 |
| Virginia | 23,116 | 18,470 | 4,646 |
| Total | 39,245 | 25,950 | 13,295 |

**Table 9—Veneer volume by destination, source, and species group, North Carolina, 2001**

| Destination and source | All species | Species group | |
|---|---|---|---|
| | | Softwood | Hardwood |
| | *thousand cubic feet* | | |
| **North Carolina (retained)** | 47,799 | 28,879 | 18,920 |
| **Exports to:** | | | |
| Georgia | 642 | 554 | 88 |
| South Carolina | 1,166 | 883 | 283 |
| Virginia | 3,812 | 3,801 | 11 |
| Total | 5,620 | 5,238 | 382 |
| **Imports from:** | | | |
| Georgia | 101 | 0 | 101 |
| Indiana | 88 | 0 | 88 |
| Kentucky | 257 | 0 | 257 |
| Maryland | 30 | 0 | 30 |
| Michigan | 24 | 0 | 24 |
| New York | 24 | 0 | 24 |
| Ohio | 125 | 0 | 125 |
| Pennsylvania | 282 | 0 | 282 |
| South Carolina | 3,882 | 3,200 | 682 |
| Tennessee | 174 | 0 | 174 |
| Virginia | 3,602 | 0 | 3,602 |
| West Virginia | 379 | 0 | 379 |
| Total | 8,968 | 3,200 | 5,768 |

**Table 10—Pulpwood volume by destination, source, and species group, North Carolina, 2001**[a]

| Destination and source | All species | Species group | |
|---|---|---|---|
| | | Softwood | Hardwood |
| | *thousand cubic feet* | | |
| **North Carolina (retained)** | 154,486 | 97,456 | 57,030 |
| **Exports to:** | | | |
| Georgia | 8 | 8 | 0 |
| Kentucky | 5,663 | 0 | 5,663 |
| Louisiana | 195 | 0 | 195 |
| Mississippi | 592 | 0 | 592 |
| South Carolina | 58,381 | 38,825 | 19,556 |
| Tennessee | 1,241 | 678 | 563 |
| Virginia | 22,435 | 4,936 | 17,499 |
| Total | 88,515 | 44,447 | 44,068 |
| **Imports from:** | | | |
| Alabama | 105 | 0 | 105 |
| Georgia | 436 | 0 | 436 |
| South Carolina | 21,308 | 17,227 | 4,081 |
| Tennessee | 5,414 | 0 | 5,414 |
| Virginia | 9,731 | 7,973 | 1,758 |
| Total | 36,994 | 25,200 | 11,794 |

[a] Includes roundwood delivered to nonpulpmills, then chipped and sold to pulpmills.

**Table 11—Composite panel volume by destination, source, and species group, North Carolina, 2001**

| Destination and source | All species | Species group | |
| --- | --- | --- | --- |
| | | Softwood | Hardwood |
| | *thousand cubic feet* | | |
| **North Carolina (retained)** | 31,627 | 22,770 | 8,857 |
| **Exports to:** | | | |
| South Carolina | 300 | 300 | 0 |
| Virginia | 3,679 | 3,522 | 157 |
| West Virginia | 188 | 18 | 170 |
| Total | 4,167 | 3,840 | 327 |
| **Imports from:** | | | |
| Virginia | 11,095 | 7,617 | 3,478 |
| Total | 11,095 | 7,617 | 3,478 |

**Table 12—Other industrial volume by destination, source, and species group, North Carolina, 2001[a]**

| Destination and source | All species | Species group | |
| --- | --- | --- | --- |
| | | Softwood | Hardwood |
| | *thousand cubic feet* | | |
| **North Carolina (retained)** | 857 | 857 | 0 |
| **Exports to:** | | | |
| Florida | 19 | 19 | 0 |
| South Carolina | 87 | 87 | 0 |
| Virginia | 74 | 52 | 22 |
| Total | 180 | 158 | 22 |
| **Imports from:** | | | |
| Virginia | 36 | 36 | 0 |
| Total | 36 | 36 | 0 |

[a] Includes poles, posts, mulch, firewood, log homes, charcoal, and all other industrial mills.

**Table 13—Primary mill residue volume by roundwood type, species group, and residue type, North Carolina, 2001**

| Roundwood type and species group | All types | Residue type | | | |
|---|---|---|---|---|---|
| | | Bark | Coarse | Sawdust | Shavings |
| | | *thousand cubic feet* | | | |
| **Saw logs** | | | | | |
| Softwood | 183,534 | 20,581 | 77,778 | 60,055 | 25,120 |
| Hardwood | 74,508 | 12,770 | 36,097 | 24,685 | 956 |
| Total | 258,042 | 33,351 | 113,875 | 84,740 | 26,076 |
| **Veneer logs** | | | | | |
| Softwood | 14,673 | 2,227 | 8,755 | 3,691 | 0 |
| Hardwood | 12,693 | 2,673 | 7,811 | 2,209 | 0 |
| Total | 27,366 | 4,900 | 16,566 | 5,900 | 0 |
| **Pulpwood** | | | | | |
| Softwood | 12,205 | 12,205 | 0 | 0 | 0 |
| Hardwood | 8,280 | 8,280 | 0 | 0 | 0 |
| Total | 20,485 | 20,485 | 0 | 0 | 0 |
| **Composite panels** | | | | | |
| Softwood | 5,057 | 5,057 | 0 | 0 | 0 |
| Hardwood | 2,771 | 2,771 | 0 | 0 | 0 |
| Total | 7,828 | 7,828 | 0 | 0 | 0 |
| **Other industrial**[a] | | | | | |
| Softwood | 703 | 589 | 114 | 0 | 0 |
| Hardwood | 0 | 0 | 0 | 0 | 0 |
| Total | 703 | 589 | 114 | 0 | 0 |
| **Total** | | | | | |
| Softwood | 216,172 | 40,659 | 86,647 | 63,746 | 25,120 |
| Hardwood | 98,252 | 26,494 | 43,908 | 26,894 | 956 |
| Total | 314,424 | 67,153 | 130,555 | 90,640 | 26,076 |

[a] Includes poles, pilings, posts, and other industrial products.

**Table 14—Disposal of residue at primary wood-using plants by product, species group, and type of residue, North Carolina, 1999 and 2001**

| Product and species group | All types 1999 | All types 2001 | Bark 1999 | Bark 2001 | Coarse 1999 | Coarse 2001 | Sawdust 1999 | Sawdust 2001 | Shavings 1999 | Shavings 2001 |
|---|---|---|---|---|---|---|---|---|---|---|
| | | | | | *thousand cubic feet* | | | | | |
| **Fiber products** | | | | | | | | | | |
| Softwood | 82,193 | 87,769 | 0 | 0 | 81,806 | 81,654 | 169 | 3,737 | 218 | 2,378 |
| Hardwood | 38,862 | 36,054 | 57 | 194 | 38,517 | 35,619 | 235 | 241 | 53 | 0 |
| Total | 121,055 | 123,823 | 57 | 194 | 120,323 | 117,273 | 404 | 3,978 | 271 | 2,378 |
| **Particleboard** | | | | | | | | | | |
| Softwood | 19,062 | 17,619 | 0 | 3 | 2,999 | 1,081 | 5,540 | 7,334 | 10,523 | 9,201 |
| Hardwood | 1,803 | 3,944 | 46 | 150 | 708 | 3,089 | 683 | 563 | 366 | 142 |
| Total | 20,865 | 21,563 | 46 | 153 | 3,707 | 4,170 | 6,223 | 7,897 | 10,889 | 9,343 |
| **Charcoal/ chemical wood** | | | | | | | | | | |
| Softwood | 1,823 | 0 | 0 | 0 | 0 | 0 | 1,823 | 0 | 0 | 0 |
| Hardwood | 0 | 0 | 0 | 0 | 0 | 0 | 0 | 0 | 0 | 0 |
| Total | 1,823 | 0 | 0 | 0 | 0 | 0 | 1,823 | 0 | 0 | 0 |
| **Sawn products** | | | | | | | | | | |
| Softwood | 536 | 2,409 | 0 | 0 | 536 | 2,409 | 0 | 0 | 0 | 0 |
| Hardwood | 575 | 222 | 0 | 0 | 575 | 222 | 0 | 0 | 0 | 0 |
| Total | 1,111 | 2,631 | 0 | 0 | 1,111 | 2,631 | 0 | 0 | 0 | 0 |
| **Fuel** | | | | | | | | | | |
| Softwood | 70,089 | 71,468 | 25,494 | 22,477 | 1,139 | 475 | 41,993 | 48,417 | 1,463 | 99 |
| Hardwood | 48,824 | 42,831 | 19,804 | 15,952 | 3,142 | 2,947 | 25,411 | 23,434 | 467 | 498 |
| Total | 118,913 | 114,299 | 45,298 | 38,429 | 4,281 | 3,422 | 67,404 | 71,851 | 1,930 | 597 |
| **Miscellaneous** | | | | | | | | | | |
| Softwood | 33,620 | 36,457 | 16,354 | 18,070 | 473 | 881 | 6,135 | 4,064 | 10,658 | 13,442 |
| Hardwood | 13,533 | 14,706 | 11,071 | 10,084 | 130 | 1,816 | 2,038 | 2,490 | 294 | 316 |
| Total | 47,153 | 51,163 | 27,425 | 28,154 | 603 | 2,697 | 8,173 | 6,554 | 10,952 | 13,758 |
| **Not used** | | | | | | | | | | |
| Softwood | 468 | 450 | 95 | 109 | 243 | 147 | 130 | 194 | 0 | 0 |
| Hardwood | 632 | 495 | 144 | 114 | 230 | 215 | 258 | 166 | 0 | 0 |
| Total | 1,100 | 945 | 239 | 223 | 473 | 362 | 388 | 360 | 0 | 0 |
| **All products** | | | | | | | | | | |
| Softwood | 207,791 | 216,172 | 41,943 | 40,659 | 87,196 | 86,647 | 55,790 | 63,746 | 22,862 | 25,120 |
| Hardwood | 104,229 | 98,252 | 31,122 | 26,494 | 43,302 | 43,908 | 28,625 | 26,894 | 1,180 | 956 |
| Total | 312,020 | 314,424 | 73,065 | 67,153 | 130,498 | 130,555 | 84,415 | 90,640 | 24,042 | 26,076 |

**Table 15—Roundwood timber products output by product and species group, Southern Coastal Plain Region of North Caroina, 1999 and 2001**

| Product and species group | Year | | | Percent change |
|---|---|---|---|---|
| | 1999 | 2001 | Change | |
| | *thousand cubic feet* | | | |
| **Saw logs** | | | | |
| Softwood | 95,204 | 92,943 | -2,261 | -2.4 |
| Hardwood | 18,232 | 14,046 | -4,186 | -23.0 |
| Total | 113,436 | 106,989 | -6,447 | -5.7 |
| **Veneer logs** | | | | |
| Softwood | 28,851 | 25,407 | -3,444 | -11.9 |
| Hardwood | 3,791 | 5,167 | 1,376 | 36.3 |
| Total | 32,642 | 30,574 | -2,068 | -6.3 |
| **Pulpwood**[a] | | | | |
| Softwood | 66,740 | 55,733 | -11,007 | -16.5 |
| Hardwood | 35,994 | 27,501 | -8,493 | -23.6 |
| Total | 102,734 | 83,234 | -19,500 | -19.0 |
| **Composite panels** | | | | |
| Softwood | 5,226 | 4,458 | -768 | -14.7 |
| Hardwood | 2,352 | 2,014 | -338 | -14.4 |
| Total | 7,578 | 6,472 | -1,106 | -14.6 |
| **Other industrial** | | | | |
| Softwood | 942 | 315 | -627 | -66.6 |
| Hardwood | 0 | 0 | 0 | -- |
| Total | 942 | 315 | -627 | -66.6 |
| **All industrial** | | | | |
| Softwood | 196,963 | 178,856 | -18,107 | -9.2 |
| Hardwood | 60,369 | 48,728 | -11,641 | -19.3 |
| Total | 257,332 | 227,584 | -29,748 | -11.6 |

-- = negligible.

[a] Includes roundwood delivered to nonpulpmills, then chipped and sold to pulpmills (1,448,000 cubic feet in 1999 and 1,576,000 cubic feet in 2001).

**Table 16—Roundwood timber products output by county, product, and species group, Southern Coastal Plain Region of North Carolina, 2001**

| County | All products | | Saw logs | | Veneer logs | | Pulpwood[a] | | Composite panels | | Other industrial | |
|---|---|---|---|---|---|---|---|---|---|---|---|---|
| | Soft-wood | Hard-wood | Soft-wood | Hard-wood | Soft-wood | Hard-wood | Soft-wood | Hard-wood | Soft-wood | Hard-wood | Soft-wood | Hard-wood |
| | *thousand cubic feet* | | | | | | | | | | | |
| Bladen | 13,480 | 4,813 | 6,370 | 1,987 | 1,449 | 174 | 5,661 | 2,652 | 0 | 0 | 0 | 0 |
| Brunswick | 17,629 | 1,317 | 7,867 | 149 | 869 | 112 | 8,780 | 1,005 | 113 | 51 | 0 | 0 |
| Columbus | 18,029 | 5,559 | 9,776 | 1,306 | 1,449 | 232 | 6,791 | 4,021 | 0 | 0 | 13 | 0 |
| Cumberland | 5,546 | 2,245 | 2,345 | 406 | 1,226 | 103 | 1,975 | 1,736 | 0 | 0 | 0 | 0 |
| Duplin | 6,310 | 2,687 | 2,680 | 511 | 1,730 | 779 | 1,279 | 1,116 | 621 | 281 | 0 | 0 |
| Greene | 2,775 | 354 | 1,233 | 0 | 865 | 104 | 508 | 174 | 169 | 76 | 0 | 0 |
| Harnett | 7,114 | 1,501 | 3,101 | 445 | 1,730 | 232 | 1,719 | 569 | 564 | 255 | 0 | 0 |
| Hoke | 3,323 | 1,134 | 1,763 | 324 | 869 | 50 | 637 | 760 | 0 | 0 | 54 | 0 |
| Johnston | 6,294 | 2,847 | 3,288 | 886 | 1,730 | 587 | 599 | 1,068 | 677 | 306 | 0 | 0 |
| Jones | 11,036 | 902 | 6,252 | 105 | 1,735 | 50 | 2,936 | 696 | 113 | 51 | 0 | 0 |
| Lee | 7,634 | 1,908 | 5,154 | 1,070 | 1,730 | 379 | 642 | 459 | 0 | 0 | 108 | 0 |
| Lenoir | 6,280 | 589 | 2,786 | 234 | 865 | 0 | 2,234 | 177 | 395 | 178 | 0 | 0 |
| Moore | 13,329 | 3,777 | 10,545 | 2,006 | 646 | 33 | 2,030 | 1,738 | 0 | 0 | 108 | 0 |
| New Hanover | 1,962 | 67 | 469 | 0 | 579 | 57 | 914 | 10 | 0 | 0 | 0 | 0 |
| Onslow | 12,866 | 1,021 | 5,655 | 269 | 865 | 253 | 6,177 | 423 | 169 | 76 | 0 | 0 |
| Pender | 10,375 | 2,874 | 4,486 | 849 | 1,159 | 330 | 4,730 | 1,695 | 0 | 0 | 0 | 0 |
| Richmond | 11,144 | 4,179 | 7,454 | 1,135 | 66 | 9 | 3,624 | 3,035 | 0 | 0 | 0 | 0 |
| Robeson | 6,606 | 5,357 | 3,481 | 1,011 | 1,159 | 210 | 1,934 | 4,136 | 0 | 0 | 32 | 0 |
| Sampson | 8,477 | 2,185 | 3,708 | 472 | 2,595 | 365 | 1,327 | 965 | 847 | 383 | 0 | 0 |
| Scotland | 4,712 | 1,153 | 2,754 | 315 | 1,226 | 67 | 732 | 771 | 0 | 0 | 0 | 0 |
| Wayne | 3,935 | 2,259 | 1,776 | 566 | 865 | 1,041 | 504 | 295 | 790 | 357 | 0 | 0 |
| All counties | 178,856 | 48,728 | 92,943 | 14,046 | 25,407 | 5,167 | 55,733 | 27,501 | 4,458 | 2,014 | 315 | 0 |

[a] Includes roundwood delivered to nonpulpmills, then chipped and sold to pulpmills (1,576,000 cubic feet in 2001).

**Table 17—Roundwood timber products output by product and species group, Northern Coastal Plain Region of North Carolina, 1999 and 2001**

| Product and species group | Year | | Change | Percent change |
|---|---|---|---|---|
| | 1999 | 2001 | | |
| | *thousand cubic feet* | | | |
| **Saw logs** | | | | |
| Softwood | 96,545 | 112,410 | 15,865 | 16.4 |
| Hardwood | 20,399 | 16,152 | -4,247 | -20.8 |
| Total | 116,944 | 128,562 | 11,618 | 9.9 |
| **Veneer logs** | | | | |
| Softwood | 7,116 | 5,914 | -1,202 | -16.9 |
| Hardwood | 5,781 | 5,790 | 9 | 0.2 |
| Total | 12,897 | 11,704 | -1,193 | -9.3 |
| **Pulpwood**[a] | | | | |
| Softwood | 63,126 | 56,566 | -6,560 | -10.4 |
| Hardwood | 25,538 | 33,619 | 8,081 | 31.6 |
| Total | 88,664 | 90,185 | 1,521 | 1.7 |
| **Composite panels** | | | | |
| Softwood | 350 | 958 | 608 | 173.7 |
| Hardwood | 158 | 432 | 274 | 173.4 |
| Total | 508 | 1,390 | 882 | 173.6 |
| **Other industrial** | | | | |
| Softwood | 206 | 0 | -206 | -100.0 |
| Hardwood | 0 | 0 | 0 | -- |
| Total | 206 | 0 | -206 | -100.0 |
| **All industrial** | | | | |
| Softwood | 167,343 | 175,848 | 8,505 | 5.1 |
| Hardwood | 51,876 | 55,993 | 4,117 | 7.9 |
| Total | 219,219 | 231,841 | 12,622 | 5.8 |

-- = negligible.

[a] Includes roundwood delivered to nonpulpmills, then chipped and sold to pulpmills (1,517,000 cubic feet in 1999 and 2,443,000 cubic feet in 2001).

**Table 18—Roundwood timber products output by county, product, and species group, Northern Coastal Plain Region of North Carolina, 2001**

| County | All products | | Saw logs | | Veneer logs | | Pulpwood[a] | | Composite panels | | Other industrial | |
|---|---|---|---|---|---|---|---|---|---|---|---|---|
| | Soft-wood | Hard-wood | Soft-wood | Hard-wood | Soft-wood | Hard-wood | Soft-wood | Hard-wood | Soft-wood | Hard-wood | Soft-wood | Hard-wood |
| | | | | | | *thousand cubic feet* | | | | | | |
| Beaufort | 23,098 | 6,342 | 17,667 | 1,001 | 0 | 142 | 5,431 | 5,199 | 0 | 0 | 0 | 0 |
| Bertie | 14,179 | 8,816 | 6,134 | 992 | 352 | 2,306 | 7,693 | 5,518 | 0 | 0 | 0 | 0 |
| Camden | 1,208 | 1,330 | 1,038 | 256 | 0 | 0 | 170 | 1,074 | 0 | 0 | 0 | 0 |
| Carteret | 8,689 | 376 | 5,180 | 0 | 0 | 6 | 3,509 | 370 | 0 | 0 | 0 | 0 |
| Chowan | 4,439 | 871 | 2,704 | 351 | 0 | 154 | 1,735 | 366 | 0 | 0 | 0 | 0 |
| Craven | 15,400 | 1,640 | 10,721 | 202 | 0 | 0 | 4,510 | 1,362 | 169 | 76 | 0 | 0 |
| Currituck | 909 | 489 | 787 | 270 | 0 | 0 | 122 | 219 | 0 | 0 | 0 | 0 |
| Dare | 17 | 21 | 12 | 5 | 0 | 0 | 5 | 16 | 0 | 0 | 0 | 0 |
| Edgecombe | 3,894 | 1,488 | 2,756 | 555 | 0 | 316 | 1,138 | 617 | 0 | 0 | 0 | 0 |
| Gates | 9,833 | 3,252 | 6,884 | 629 | 365 | 81 | 2,584 | 2,542 | 0 | 0 | 0 | 0 |
| Halifax | 10,314 | 5,342 | 7,516 | 3,295 | 550 | 596 | 2,248 | 1,451 | 0 | 0 | 0 | 0 |
| Hertford | 11,224 | 3,505 | 7,920 | 921 | 413 | 93 | 2,891 | 2,491 | 0 | 0 | 0 | 0 |
| Hyde | 5,062 | 1,436 | 3,605 | 386 | 0 | 0 | 1,457 | 1,050 | 0 | 0 | 0 | 0 |
| Martin | 6,593 | 2,288 | 3,517 | 901 | 0 | 35 | 3,076 | 1,352 | 0 | 0 | 0 | 0 |
| Nash | 4,540 | 3,684 | 3,712 | 1,802 | 0 | 1,420 | 659 | 386 | 169 | 76 | 0 | 0 |
| Northampton | 7,578 | 5,008 | 4,086 | 2,587 | 774 | 128 | 2,718 | 2,293 | 0 | 0 | 0 | 0 |
| Pamlico | 8,144 | 2,026 | 4,798 | 68 | 865 | 0 | 2,481 | 1,958 | 0 | 0 | 0 | 0 |
| Pasquotank | 2,280 | 795 | 1,952 | 252 | 0 | 0 | 328 | 543 | 0 | 0 | 0 | 0 |
| Perquimans | 4,736 | 778 | 3,596 | 225 | 0 | 0 | 1,140 | 553 | 0 | 0 | 0 | 0 |
| Pitt | 6,631 | 966 | 3,577 | 197 | 0 | 0 | 2,829 | 667 | 225 | 102 | 0 | 0 |
| Tyrrell | 7,099 | 2,764 | 4,327 | 382 | 0 | 91 | 2,772 | 2,291 | 0 | 0 | 0 | 0 |
| Washington | 13,442 | 1,540 | 7,555 | 438 | 0 | 0 | 5,887 | 1,102 | 0 | 0 | 0 | 0 |
| Wilson | 6,539 | 1,236 | 2,366 | 437 | 2,595 | 422 | 1,183 | 199 | 395 | 178 | 0 | 0 |
| All counties | 175,848 | 55,993 | 112,410 | 16,152 | 5,914 | 5,790 | 56,566 | 33,619 | 958 | 432 | 0 | 0 |

[a] Includes roundwood delivered to nonpulpmills, then chipped and sold to pulpmills (2,443,000 cubic feet in 2001).

**Table 19—Roundwood timber products output by product and species group, Piedmont Region of North Carolina, 1999 and 2001**

| Product and species group | Year | | | Percent change |
|---|---|---|---|---|
| | 1999 | 2001 | Change | |
| | *thousand cubic feet* | | | |
| **Saw logs** | | | | |
| Softwood | 83,901 | 84,477 | 576 | 0.7 |
| Hardwood | 55,990 | 54,933 | -1,057 | -1.9 |
| Total | 139,891 | 139,410 | -481 | -0.3 |
| **Veneer logs** | | | | |
| Softwood | 5,625 | 2,238 | -3,387 | -60.2 |
| Hardwood | 5,994 | 5,168 | -826 | -13.8 |
| Total | 11,619 | 7,406 | -4,213 | -36.3 |
| **Pulpwood**[a] | | | | |
| Softwood | 29,840 | 25,127 | -4,713 | -15.8 |
| Hardwood | 31,975 | 24,493 | -7,482 | -23.4 |
| Total | 61,815 | 49,620 | -12,195 | -19.7 |
| **Composite panels** | | | | |
| Softwood | 20,947 | 19,645 | -1,302 | -6.2 |
| Hardwood | 5,598 | 6,464 | 866 | 15.5 |
| Total | 26,545 | 26,109 | -436 | -1.6 |
| **Other industrial** | | | | |
| Softwood | 504 | 628 | 124 | 24.6 |
| Hardwood | 0 | 22 | 22 | -- |
| Total | 504 | 650 | 146 | 29.0 |
| **All industrial** | | | | |
| Softwood | 140,817 | 132,115 | -8,702 | -6.2 |
| Hardwood | 99,557 | 91,080 | -8,477 | -8.5 |
| Total | 240,374 | 223,195 | -17,179 | -7.1 |

-- = negligible.

[a] Includes roundwood delivered to nonpulpmills, then chipped and sold to pulpmills (3,172,000 cubic feet in 1999 and 3,365,000 cubic feet in 2001).

Table 20—Roundwood timber products output by county, product, and species group, Piedmont Region of North Carolina, 2001

| County | All products | | Saw logs | | Veneer logs | | Pulpwood[a] | | Composite panels | | Other industrial | |
| --- | --- | --- | --- | --- | --- | --- | --- | --- | --- | --- | --- | --- |
| | Soft-wood | Hard-wood | Soft-wood | Hard-wood | Soft-wood | Hard-wood | Soft-wood | Hard-wood | Soft-wood | Hard-wood | Soft-wood | Hard-wood |
| | *thousand cubic feet* | | | | | | | | | | | |
| Alamance | 2,124 | 2,628 | 2,014 | 2,489 | 0 | 0 | 1 | 34 | 109 | 105 | 0 | 0 |
| Alexander | 1,141 | 846 | 1,021 | 711 | 0 | 98 | 101 | 37 | 0 | 0 | 19 | 0 |
| Anson | 19,844 | 3,094 | 13,547 | 1,242 | 563 | 90 | 5,734 | 1,762 | 0 | 0 | 0 | 0 |
| Cabarrus | 1,370 | 507 | 1,100 | 471 | 0 | 0 | 161 | 36 | 109 | 0 | 0 | 0 |
| Caswell | 4,375 | 4,157 | 1,822 | 2,184 | 0 | 360 | 15 | 979 | 2,538 | 634 | 0 | 0 |
| Catawba | 1,550 | 706 | 1,365 | 575 | 0 | 35 | 76 | 96 | 109 | 0 | 0 | 0 |
| Chatham | 9,864 | 5,719 | 7,528 | 3,863 | 0 | 911 | 1,425 | 549 | 799 | 396 | 112 | 0 |
| Cleveland | 2,104 | 643 | 622 | 430 | 0 | 18 | 826 | 90 | 656 | 105 | 0 | 0 |
| Davidson | 2,827 | 4,196 | 2,236 | 3,554 | 0 | 32 | 263 | 452 | 328 | 158 | 0 | 0 |
| Davie | 1,087 | 1,000 | 896 | 765 | 0 | 9 | 78 | 121 | 109 | 105 | 4 | 0 |
| Durham | 3,061 | 3,018 | 1,956 | 183 | 0 | 22 | 416 | 2,596 | 689 | 217 | 0 | 0 |
| Forsyth | 818 | 1,334 | 568 | 1,086 | 0 | 4 | 12 | 127 | 219 | 117 | 19 | 0 |
| Franklin | 4,881 | 3,833 | 3,661 | 1,594 | 350 | 265 | 870 | 1,974 | 0 | 0 | 0 | 0 |
| Gaston | 1,007 | 387 | 298 | 23 | 0 | 3 | 600 | 309 | 109 | 52 | 0 | 0 |
| Granville | 5,521 | 1,479 | 4,001 | 813 | 43 | 370 | 278 | 91 | 1,020 | 205 | 179 | 0 |
| Guilford | 944 | 2,111 | 819 | 1,951 | 0 | 4 | 16 | 104 | 109 | 52 | 0 | 0 |
| Iredell | 2,568 | 1,454 | 2,060 | 1,053 | 0 | 50 | 277 | 193 | 219 | 158 | 12 | 0 |
| Lincoln | 1,434 | 713 | 824 | 304 | 0 | 54 | 501 | 355 | 109 | 0 | 0 | 0 |
| Mecklenburg | 581 | 1,203 | 384 | 805 | 0 | 45 | 88 | 301 | 109 | 52 | 0 | 0 |
| Montgomery | 10,881 | 3,618 | 8,074 | 3,178 | 0 | 0 | 2,698 | 440 | 109 | 0 | 0 | 0 |
| Orange | 1,735 | 1,723 | 1,323 | 843 | 0 | 427 | 193 | 85 | 219 | 368 | 0 | 0 |
| Person | 4,452 | 1,959 | 2,060 | 844 | 0 | 360 | 38 | 244 | 2,319 | 489 | 35 | 22 |
| Polk | 665 | 846 | 383 | 842 | 0 | 0 | 173 | 4 | 102 | 0 | 7 | 0 |
| Randolph | 3,900 | 5,478 | 3,124 | 4,822 | 0 | 72 | 448 | 426 | 328 | 158 | 0 | 0 |
| Rockingham | 5,138 | 5,872 | 1,920 | 3,210 | 86 | 191 | 440 | 1,511 | 2,692 | 960 | 0 | 0 |
| Rowan | 1,965 | 2,547 | 1,206 | 2,163 | 0 | 9 | 322 | 375 | 437 | 0 | 0 | 0 |
| Rutherford | 3,600 | 7,067 | 2,020 | 1,381 | 0 | 0 | 945 | 5,686 | 635 | 0 | 0 | 0 |
| Stanly | 2,766 | 1,161 | 1,631 | 1,000 | 0 | 0 | 807 | 161 | 328 | 0 | 0 | 0 |
| Stokes | 1,446 | 2,899 | 857 | 1,948 | 0 | 0 | 13 | 573 | 547 | 378 | 29 | 0 |
| Surry | 2,547 | 2,942 | 1,915 | 2,167 | 0 | 0 | 35 | 397 | 547 | 378 | 50 | 0 |
| Union | 2,108 | 1,054 | 225 | 457 | 320 | 59 | 1,454 | 486 | 109 | 52 | 0 | 0 |
| Vance | 4,385 | 1,943 | 1,616 | 770 | 350 | 601 | 255 | 100 | 2,110 | 472 | 54 | 0 |
| Wake | 6,044 | 3,066 | 4,396 | 1,599 | 0 | 350 | 534 | 535 | 1,025 | 582 | 89 | 0 |
| Warren | 10,888 | 6,988 | 4,668 | 3,136 | 526 | 729 | 5,005 | 2,906 | 689 | 217 | 0 | 0 |
| Yadkin | 2,494 | 2,889 | 2,337 | 2,477 | 0 | 0 | 29 | 358 | 109 | 54 | 19 | 0 |
| All counties | 132,115 | 91,080 | 84,477 | 54,933 | 2,238 | 5,168 | 25,127 | 24,493 | 19,645 | 6,464 | 628 | 22 |

[a] Includes roundwood delivered to nonpulpmills, then chipped and sold to pulpmills (3,365,000 cubic feet in 2001).

**Table 21—Roundwood timber products output by product and species group, Mountain Region of North Carolina, 1999 and 2001**

| Product and species group | Year 1999 | 2001 | Change | Percent change |
|---|---|---|---|---|
| | *thousand cubic feet* | | | |
| **Saw logs** | | | | |
| Softwood | 20,640 | 18,838 | -1,802 | -8.7 |
| Hardwood | 31,157 | 31,450 | 293 | 0.9 |
| Total | 51,797 | 50,288 | -1,509 | -2.9 |
| **Veneer logs** | | | | |
| Softwood | 156 | 558 | 402 | 257.7 |
| Hardwood | 3,744 | 3,177 | -567 | -15.1 |
| Total | 3,900 | 3,735 | -165 | -4.2 |
| **Pulpwood[a]** | | | | |
| Softwood | 5,285 | 4,477 | -808 | -15.3 |
| Hardwood | 13,347 | 15,485 | 2,138 | 16.0 |
| Total | 18,632 | 19,962 | 1,330 | 7.1 |
| **Composite panels** | | | | |
| Softwood | 927 | 1,549 | 622 | 67.1 |
| Hardwood | 752 | 274 | -478 | -63.6 |
| Total | 1,679 | 1,823 | 144 | 8.6 |
| **Other industrial** | | | | |
| Softwood | 126 | 72 | -54 | -42.9 |
| Hardwood | 0 | 0 | 0 | -- |
| Total | 126 | 72 | -54 | -42.9 |
| **All industrial** | | | | |
| Softwood | 27,134 | 25,494 | -1,640 | -6.0 |
| Hardwood | 49,000 | 50,386 | 1,386 | 2.8 |
| Total | 76,134 | 75,880 | -254 | -0.3 |

-- = negligible.

[a] Includes roundwood delivered to nonpulpmills, then chipped and sold to pulpmills (1,232,000 cubic feet in 1999 and 362,000 cubic feet in 2001).

**Table 22—Roundwood timber products output by county, product, and species group, Mountain Region of North Carolina, 2001**

| County | All products | | Saw logs | | Veneer logs | | Pulpwood[a] | | Composite panels | | Other industrial | |
|---|---|---|---|---|---|---|---|---|---|---|---|---|
| | Soft-wood | Hard-wood | Soft-wood | Hard-wood | Soft-wood | Hard-wood | Soft-wood | Hard-wood | Soft-wood | Hard-wood | Soft-wood | Hard-wood |
| | *thousand cubic feet* | | | | | | | | | | | |
| Alleghany | 1,098 | 1,298 | 1,021 | 985 | 0 | 45 | 25 | 268 | 0 | 0 | 52 | 0 |
| Ashe | 1,639 | 2,181 | 1,601 | 1,649 | 0 | 56 | 20 | 306 | 18 | 170 | 0 | 0 |
| Avery | 619 | 1,628 | 619 | 1,482 | 0 | 108 | 0 | 38 | 0 | 0 | 0 | 0 |
| Buncombe | 792 | 1,838 | 792 | 1,676 | 0 | 162 | 0 | 0 | 0 | 0 | 0 | 0 |
| Burke | 5,265 | 4,871 | 2,708 | 1,736 | 0 | 82 | 1,572 | 3,001 | 985 | 52 | 0 | 0 |
| Caldwell | 2,512 | 2,437 | 2,366 | 1,865 | 0 | 172 | 37 | 400 | 109 | 0 | 0 | 0 |
| Cherokee | 1,584 | 3,164 | 471 | 706 | 0 | 93 | 1,113 | 2,365 | 0 | 0 | 0 | 0 |
| Clay | 7 | 171 | 7 | 171 | 0 | 0 | 0 | 0 | 0 | 0 | 0 | 0 |
| Graham | 132 | 769 | 132 | 453 | 0 | 316 | 0 | 0 | 0 | 0 | 0 | 0 |
| Haywood | 1,802 | 8,539 | 142 | 2,297 | 0 | 153 | 1,660 | 6,089 | 0 | 0 | 0 | 0 |
| Henderson | 985 | 777 | 984 | 615 | 0 | 162 | 1 | 0 | 0 | 0 | 0 | 0 |
| Jackson | 264 | 1,311 | 264 | 1,203 | 0 | 108 | 0 | 0 | 0 | 0 | 0 | 0 |
| Macon | 147 | 1,057 | 147 | 911 | 0 | 146 | 0 | 0 | 0 | 0 | 0 | 0 |
| Madison | 992 | 3,786 | 992 | 3,137 | 0 | 649 | 0 | 0 | 0 | 0 | 0 | 0 |
| McDowell | 843 | 1,378 | 726 | 1,193 | 0 | 136 | 8 | 49 | 109 | 0 | 0 | 0 |
| Mitchell | 852 | 2,362 | 848 | 2,146 | 4 | 216 | 0 | 0 | 0 | 0 | 0 | 0 |
| Swain | 720 | 764 | 166 | 679 | 554 | 85 | 0 | 0 | 0 | 0 | 0 | 0 |
| Transylvania | 58 | 205 | 58 | 205 | 0 | 0 | 0 | 0 | 0 | 0 | 0 | 0 |
| Watauga | 1,390 | 1,713 | 1,390 | 1,552 | 0 | 0 | 0 | 161 | 0 | 0 | 0 | 0 |
| Wilkes | 3,099 | 7,122 | 2,710 | 4,153 | 0 | 109 | 41 | 2,808 | 328 | 52 | 20 | 0 |
| Yancey | 694 | 3,015 | 694 | 2,636 | 0 | 379 | 0 | 0 | 0 | 0 | 0 | 0 |
| All counties | 25,494 | 50,386 | 18,838 | 31,450 | 558 | 3,177 | 4,477 | 15,485 | 1,549 | 274 | 72 | 0 |

[a] Includes roundwood delivered to nonpulpmills, then chipped and sold to pulpmills (362,000 cubic feet in 2001).

**Table 23—Total roundwood output by product, species group, and source of material, North Carolina, 2001**

| Product and species group | All sources | Total | Growing-stock trees | | Other sources |
| | | | Sawtimber | Poletimber | |
|---|---|---|---|---|---|
| | | | *thousand cubic feet* | | |
| **Saw logs** | | | | | |
| Softwood | 308,668 | 303,888 | 296,004 | 7,884 | 4,780 |
| Hardwood | 116,581 | 115,347 | 107,887 | 7,460 | 1,234 |
| Total | 425,249 | 419,235 | 403,891 | 15,344 | 6,014 |
| **Veneer logs and bolts** | | | | | |
| Softwood | 34,117 | 33,466 | 32,459 | 1,007 | 651 |
| Hardwood | 19,302 | 19,086 | 19,086 | 0 | 216 |
| Total | 53,419 | 52,552 | 51,545 | 1,007 | 867 |
| **Pulpwood** | | | | | |
| Softwood | 141,903 | 135,679 | 50,358 | 85,321 | 6,224 |
| Hardwood | 101,098 | 99,076 | 31,960 | 67,116 | 2,022 |
| Total | 243,001 | 234,755 | 82,318 | 152,437 | 8,246 |
| **Composite panels** | | | | | |
| Softwood | 26,610 | 26,211 | 7,145 | 19,066 | 399 |
| Hardwood | 9,184 | 8,804 | 4,987 | 3,817 | 380 |
| Total | 35,794 | 35,015 | 12,132 | 22,883 | 779 |
| **Poles and posts** | | | | | |
| Softwood | 996 | 740 | 397 | 343 | 256 |
| Hardwood | 0 | 0 | 0 | 0 | 0 |
| Total | 996 | 740 | 397 | 343 | 256 |
| **Other miscellaneous** | | | | | |
| Softwood | 19 | 16 | 8 | 7 | 3 |
| Hardwood | 22 | 22 | 9 | 13 | 0 |
| Total | 41 | 38 | 17 | 20 | 3 |
| **Total industrial products** | | | | | |
| Softwood | 512,313 | 500,000 | 386,372 | 113,628 | 12,313 |
| Hardwood | 246,187 | 242,335 | 163,929 | 78,406 | 3,852 |
| Total | 758,500 | 742,335 | 550,301 | 192,034 | 16,165 |
| **Fuelwood** | | | | | |
| Softwood | 9,584 | 8,490 | 4,936 | 3,554 | 1,094 |
| Hardwood | 80,330 | 69,468 | 50,814 | 18,655 | 10,862 |
| Total | 89,914 | 77,958 | 55,750 | 22,209 | 11,956 |
| **All products** | | | | | |
| Softwood | 521,897 | 508,490 | 391,308 | 117,182 | 13,407 |
| Hardwood | 326,517 | 311,803 | 214,743 | 97,061 | 14,714 |
| Total | 848,414 | 820,293 | 606,050 | 214,243 | 28,121 |

Numbers in rows and columns may not sum to totals due to rounding.

**Table 24—Total roundwood output by species group, survey region, and
ownership class, North Carolina, 2001**

| Species group and survey region | Total | Ownership class | | |
|---|---|---|---|---|
| | | Public | Forest industry | Nonindustrial private |
| | | *thousand cubic feet* | | |
| **Softwoods** | | | | |
| Southern Coastal Plain | 182,202 | 15,206 | 38,385 | 128,610 |
| Northern Coastal Plain | 179,138 | 522 | 68,053 | 110,563 |
| Piedmont | 134,585 | 1,306 | 8,082 | 125,198 |
| Mountain | 25,972 | 3,600 | 868 | 21,504 |
| Total softwoods | 521,897 | 20,634 | 115,388 | 385,875 |
| **Hardwoods** | | | | |
| Southern Coastal Plain | 64,628 | 1,120 | 9,426 | 54,082 |
| Northern Coastal Plain | 74,264 | 445 | 9,273 | 64,546 |
| Piedmont | 120,797 | 869 | 1,601 | 118,327 |
| Mountain | 66,828 | 4,209 | 366 | 62,253 |
| Total hardwoods | 326,517 | 6,642 | 20,666 | 299,208 |
| **All species** | 848,414 | 27,277 | 136,054 | 685,083 |

Numbers in rows and columns may not sum to totals due to rounding.

**Table 25—Total roundwood output by species group, detailed species group, and product, North Carolina, 2001**

| Species group and detailed species group | Total | Saw log | Veneer | Pulpwood | Composite panel | Poles and posts | Other miscellaneous | Fuel-wood |
|---|---|---|---|---|---|---|---|---|
| | | | | *thousand cubic feet* | | | | |
| **Softwood** | | | | | | | | |
| Cedar | 2,387 | 1,441 | 135 | 375 | 378 | 15 | 0 | 44 |
| Longleaf-slash pine | 30,064 | 15,291 | 3,309 | 10,586 | 250 | 74 | 2 | 552 |
| White pine | 14,842 | 10,331 | 4 | 3,143 | 1,028 | 63 | 0 | 274 |
| Loblolly-shortleaf pine | 410,654 | 241,501 | 28,661 | 114,812 | 17,430 | 696 | 14 | 7,540 |
| Other yellow pines | 59,275 | 37,565 | 1,579 | 11,470 | 7,421 | 148 | 3 | 1,089 |
| Cypress | 4,214 | 2,155 | 428 | 1,452 | 100 | 0 | 0 | 77 |
| Hemlock | 461 | 384 | 0 | 66 | 3 | 0 | 0 | 8 |
| Total softwoods | 521,897 | 308,668 | 34,117 | 141,903 | 26,610 | 996 | 19 | 9,584 |
| **Hardwood** | | | | | | | | |
| Soft maple | 33,987 | 11,019 | 2,051 | 11,761 | 791 | 0 | 3 | 8,361 |
| Hard maple | 969 | 337 | 13 | 368 | 13 | 0 | 0 | 239 |
| Other birch | 1,397 | 618 | 77 | 335 | 24 | 0 | 0 | 344 |
| Yellow birch | 748 | 242 | 12 | 299 | 10 | 0 | 0 | 184 |
| Hickory | 13,290 | 5,622 | 595 | 3,422 | 380 | 0 | 1 | 3,270 |
| Beech | 3,001 | 1,595 | 164 | 414 | 90 | 0 | 0 | 739 |
| Ash | 5,728 | 2,980 | 175 | 979 | 185 | 0 | 0 | 1,409 |
| Black walnut | 588 | 307 | 32 | 66 | 38 | 0 | 0 | 145 |
| Sweetgum | 43,598 | 10,809 | 3,427 | 17,271 | 1,358 | 0 | 7 | 10,726 |
| Yellow-poplar | 71,146 | 27,716 | 3,790 | 20,151 | 1,983 | 0 | 3 | 17,504 |
| Blackgum-tupelo | 12,305 | 2,911 | 1,043 | 5,101 | 222 | 0 | 0 | 3,027 |
| Sycamore | 559 | 304 | 29 | 87 | 1 | 0 | 0 | 138 |
| Cottonwood | 170 | 68 | 29 | 31 | 1 | 0 | 0 | 42 |
| Black cherry | 1,933 | 603 | 48 | 759 | 48 | 0 | 0 | 476 |
| Select white oaks | 38,590 | 14,417 | 2,177 | 11,119 | 1,379 | 0 | 4 | 9,494 |
| Other white oaks | 13,463 | 6,222 | 541 | 2,938 | 447 | 0 | 2 | 3,312 |
| Select red oaks | 12,515 | 4,844 | 872 | 3,429 | 290 | 0 | 1 | 3,078 |
| Other red oaks | 50,229 | 16,892 | 3,191 | 16,383 | 1,405 | 0 | 1 | 12,357 |
| Basswood | 1,815 | 653 | 51 | 658 | 7 | 0 | 0 | 447 |
| Elm | 2,262 | 815 | 134 | 667 | 90 | 0 | 0 | 556 |
| Other Eastern hardwoods | 18,224 | 7,608 | 851 | 4,859 | 423 | 0 | 0 | 4,483 |
| Total hardwoods | 326,517 | 116,581 | 19,302 | 101,098 | 9,184 | 0 | 22 | 80,330 |
| **All species** | 848,414 | 425,249 | 53,419 | 243,001 | 35,794 | 996 | 41 | 89,914 |

Numbers in rows and columns may not sum to totals due to rounding.

**Table 26—Total roundwood output by species group, detailed species group, and ownership class, North Carolina, 2001**

| Species group and detailed species group | Total | Ownership class | | |
|---|---|---|---|---|
| | | Public | Forest industry | Nonindustrial private |
| | | *thousand cubic feet* | | |
| **Softwood** | | | | |
| Cedar | 2,387 | 77 | 291 | 2,018 |
| Longleaf-slash pine | 30,064 | 2,016 | 9,506 | 18,542 |
| White pine | 14,842 | 2,842 | 868 | 11,133 |
| Loblolly-shortleaf pine | 410,654 | 13,698 | 97,775 | 299,182 |
| Other yellow pines | 59,275 | 1,924 | 5,706 | 51,644 |
| Cypress | 4,214 | 3 | 1,241 | 2,969 |
| Hemlock | 461 | 74 | 0 | 387 |
| Total softwoods | 521,897 | 20,634 | 115,388 | 385,875 |
| **Hardwood** | | | | |
| Soft maple | 33,987 | 553 | 2,777 | 30,657 |
| Hard maple | 969 | 0 | 0 | 969 |
| Other birch | 1,397 | 44 | 30 | 1,323 |
| Yellow birch | 748 | 6 | 10 | 732 |
| Hickory | 13,290 | 251 | 341 | 12,698 |
| Beech | 3,001 | 44 | 99 | 2,858 |
| Ash | 5,728 | 53 | 252 | 5,423 |
| Black walnut | 588 | 4 | 0 | 584 |
| Sweetgum | 43,598 | 382 | 4,200 | 39,015 |
| Yellow-poplar | 71,146 | 665 | 3,275 | 67,206 |
| Blackgum-tupelo | 12,305 | 74 | 2,122 | 10,110 |
| Sycamore | 559 | 4 | 5 | 551 |
| Cottonwood | 170 | 5 | 3 | 162 |
| Black cherry | 1,933 | 17 | 104 | 1,812 |
| Select white oaks | 38,590 | 1,088 | 1,580 | 35,922 |
| Other white oaks | 13,463 | 576 | 348 | 12,539 |
| Select red oaks | 12,515 | 606 | 394 | 11,515 |
| Other red oaks | 50,229 | 1,795 | 3,904 | 44,529 |
| Basswood | 1,815 | 33 | 24 | 1,758 |
| Elm | 2,262 | 8 | 128 | 2,125 |
| Other Eastern hardwoods | 18,224 | 433 | 1,071 | 16,719 |
| Total hardwoods | 326,517 | 6,642 | 20,666 | 299,208 |
| **All species** | 848,414 | 27,277 | 136,054 | 685,083 |

Numbers in rows and columns may not sum to totals due to rounding.